DUE DILIGENCE
AND THE NEWS

"This formidable censor [the newspaper press] of the public functionaries, by arraigning them at the tribunal of public opinion, produces reform peaceably, which must otherwise be done by revolution."

—Thomas Jefferson

DUE DILIGENCE AND THE NEWS

Searching for a Moral Compass in the Digital Age

STANLEY E. FLINK

Center for Media and Journalism Studies at Indian River State College

ISBN 978-0-578-60291-2

Presented in conjunction with the Center for Media and Journalism Studies at Indian River State College, 3209 Virginia Avenue, Fort Pierce, Florida, 34981.

IRSC CENTER FOR
Media & Journalism
STUDIES

For information on supplementary instructional materials, please contact Dr. Bruce W. Fraser, Professor of Humanities, Indian River State College. 3209 Virginia Avenue, Fort Pierce, Florida, 34981.

Printed by Gorham Printing, 3718 Mahoney Drive, Centralia, WA 98512

For those dedicated men and women of journalism
who seek the truth, as best they can,
even when their own safety is at risk.

⟿

Contents

꞊

꞊

CONGRESS shall make no law respecting an establishment of religion, or prohibiting the free exercise thereof; or abridging the freedom of speech, or of the press; or the right of the people peaceably to assemble, and to petition the Government for a redress of grievances.

—First Amendment
The Constitution of the United States

Acknowledgement

My conviction is that freedom of the press will survive only if a large proportion of the citizenry is willing to watch over it. This will require surveillance, fact finding and education.

The essays in this collection were informed by years of research and teaching about public affairs journalism, at both New York University and Yale University.

When my wife and I began to spend more time in Florida, I was able to develop a relationship with the Center for Media Studies and Journalism at Indian River State College, which is located in Fort Pierce, Florida, not far from where we lived.

The Center is the kind of enterprise that will help people in the nearby communities and beyond to understand the nature and purpose of a free press, and to value its contributions to democracy.

I am particularly grateful to Professor Bruce Fraser for his work as a founder of the Center, and his insightful commentary on my essays. An institution such as IRSC, and its student body and faculty, can bring the energy and curiosity of a diverse group of people to the issues of technology and political manipulation that afflict the modern media.

  This book is dedicated to journalists, but it aspires to help the consumers of journalistic reporting and opinion to evaluate the contents of what they read and watch with a knowledgeable perception of truth-telling integrity. I am grateful for the opportunity to share in their ruminations.

Stanley E. Flink

October 2019

Foreword

IN THE SPRING of 2006, Stanley Flink descended on Indian River State College to inaugurate a series of lectures through what would later become the Feilden Institute of Lifelong Learning. That opening lecture, titled "Protecting America's Newsrooms," became the focus of what would evolve into a 12-year conversation between Stan and me about the nature and role of the press in a rapidly changing world, one that had seen the birth of the desktop computer in the previous century and the rise of the Internet in the preceding decade. Times were changing, and journalism was struggling to keep up. What was at stake was the future of the Fourth Estate itself, as online journalism—much of it generated by small operations or ambitious individuals—was encroaching increasingly on the territory and profit margins of established print news organizations. Ideas about knowledge and communication were shifting, and public discourse was sliding into increasingly vitriolic, partisan squabbling. Print journalism seemed moribund, and the worry was—and is—that what would take its place could not serve the public interest in ways necessary for the preservation of our democracy. The clamoring and sometimes raucous voices amplifying across the Internet seem more divisive than communitarian, more likely to make communication and truth less prominent than more.

The focus of this conversation oscillated between theory and practice, Stanley's background as a journalist challenging and grounding my predilections as a philosopher, and my interest in abstract questions about knowledge, evidence, and truth informing his own views on the future of journalism. The result was the birth of IRSC's Center for Media and Journalism Studies, a collaboration of faculty and students committed to raising public awareness of the role of journalism in the digital age, and to providing carefully vetted information about issues in the public interest.

The model for the Center was intriguing but not new. Walter Lippmann, media critic and journalist (discussed at length in the essays that follow) had proposed something similar in his 1922 book *Public Opinion*, a prophetic and insightful analysis of the challenges facing the news business in an increasingly technological society. Concerned by the flood of information that would swamp the public sphere and force people back into their subjective preferences and biases, Lippmann proposed that an objective group of experts vet the information and provide concise, actionable analyses of the day's events and issues to public officials and the media– not unlike the role of the Congressional Research

Office, which provides this kind of analysis for legislators. Lippmann had hoped to bring the expertise of academe to bear on the news, providing a filter for the flow of information to the public that would allow people to make informed decisions about the business of managing their lives. The Center, in a much more modest role, attempted to do the same by linking the college classroom to the public domain in a way that engaged students with important issues and shared their findings with the community. In this way, the decline of the modern newsroom, with its attendant function of vetting stories and providing essential context and analysis, could be remedied to some extent by connecting journalism with the learning objectives of college courses. It would also prepare students for the world beyond the classroom, cultivating what we refer to as 'due diligence,' i.e., the capacity and wherewithal of private citizens to evaluate information for both truth and relevance—and, it is hoped, to assess its moral implications.

From 2008 onward, Indian River State College's Media Center vested itself in the effort to engage students from a variety of backgrounds with America's free press. In the subsequent decade, it became clear that two central themes must guide this effort to improve the public's understanding of, and engagement with, the news: due diligence, and the need to connect the content of college-level instruction to public life. Personal responsibility and education—hardly novel solutions to what is arguably the greatest challenge to our democracy since its founding, viz., the preservation of public information that makes self-governance possible. But it is the solution that makes most sense as a stopgap to the slide into technological tribalism.

The reflections that follow represent the culmination of this work through and for IRSC's Center for Media and Journalism Studies. Each topic, each essay, was developed with a broad readership in mind—and with an eye to providing essential history and context for understanding the changing landscape of America's free press. The topics can be taken as part of an extended narrative, but they can also be considered as freestanding provocations. None is meant to be the last word, but all are meant to inspire some level of engagement with what is arguably the most pressing issue of our time: how to separate truth from falsehood, fiction, and propaganda. In a sense, these reflections form a constellation of historical and philosophical perspectives, woven together with journalistic skill in the hope of reviving an interest in healthy public dialogue and engagement. The future of our democracy depends, as it always has, on a viable Fourth Estate, and truth is the ground on which that Estate is founded. *Due Diligence and the News* represents a serious but accessible effort to present the defining issues of our time in a way that engages the reader and encourages an informed evaluation of journalism and the media.

Much of the research for these essays was completed for an earlier publication by Stanley Flink: *Sentinel Under Siege:*

The Triumphs and Troubles of America's Free Press (Harper Collins, 1998)—a thoroughly researched book on the history and evolution of the American press. For those readers interested in a thoroughgoing scholarly treatment of the content, a careful read of *Sentinel* will not disappoint. Additional resources used in the development of this work are mentioned explicitly in the text itself.

Bruce W. Fraser
Indian River State College

Preface

DEMOCRACY HAS NO life without truth, and the process of truth-seeking has little hope of succeeding in a diverse society without a free and independent press.

The ruminations in this collection of essays examine the dramatic history of journalism as a part of the American experience since the beginning of government in the colonial settlements. Now, in the 21st century, we confront the fact that the concept of determining truth, based on evidence and education, can no longer be assured.

The Internet, as we know, entered our lives bright with promise and wonder. But we have also seen its capacity for distortion and falsehood. Cynical and corrupt manipulators, including merchants of hate and division, have harnessed Internet technologies and used them to deceive and reshape public perception. They have attached misinformation to the fears and prejudices of a large segment of the American electorate and captured voter sentiments that have lingered just below the surface of political calculations for several decades. Among those sentiments are the resentment and confusion that accompany loss of manufacturing jobs, and the demographic shifts in the population around them. Some of these tremors are understandable, others are sinister and contradict the deepest principles of the Constitution.

The remedies—if there are any—require public awareness, truthful rendering of the facts, and the willingness to change our minds. The Founders recommended that liberty be protected by vigilance, but the power of the Internet was not imaginable in 1787. The willing belief in presuppositions has always been part of the body politic, but influencing millions of citizens almost overnight, and repetitively, is a phenomenon few people could anticipate. The structure of persuasion has been corrupted by deliberate falsehood, and targeted malevolent propaganda, able to reach voters swiftly, over and over.

The planning for what became the United States could not have predicted the digital revolution. Those who invented it, in fact, are not yet sure of their vision. It will take dedicated hard work, education and due diligence to help the public in the process of auditing information systems that can inflict such compelling powers of misinformation without statutory restraints, or the ability to recall or countermand automated information "bots." The damage that can be done is currently beyond control. At risk is democracy itself.

Looked at in terms of defensive actions, the due diligence concept adapts common sense measures. It begins with understanding the indisputable decline in respect for the truth. The massive explosion of information providers, and the corruption of news about public affairs by deliberate falsehoods online, has created the option to select whatever version of reality pleases us the most—despite the facts. By influencing public perception with the help of personal data "harvested" from competitive platforms, people with no interest in the truth have been able to target potential voters. Misinformation can effect voting decisions. Once truth becomes irrelevant, the manipulation of public opinion becomes not only likely but more deceptive.

The consumer of news has to find conveyors of news he or she can trust. Journalism will be validated by unfolding events. The trustworthy providers earn their places in print, television and online by careful research and affirmation. Fact-checking services are available, and more of them will appear in the coming years—particularly as critical elections and political campaigns are amplified. The 2016 presidential election widened the field for fact-checking along with the revelations on data harvesting.

Some consumers will take the time to compare reporting in competing newspapers or electronic communications. Consciousness about the misuse of data, and "fake news," may have some positive consequences—among them greater care in preparing news materials, and less willing belief in false stories. If the competing sources of news find that demonstrable truth-telling in the news business is a good investment, the machinations of miscreant "trolls" working on deception may diminish.

Whatever the trend may be over time, news will always be controversial if only because those who produce it bring different perspectives to the enterprise. For this reason alone a comparison of sources, and frequent reliance on fact-checkers, internally and externally, should become routine. It seems predictable that new companies—mostly online—will engage a growing audience in determining where truth based on facts is most likely to be found, and who specifically are the truth tellers.

Perhaps a major commission can be formed that will have the prestige and expertise necessary to monitor truth-telling and accountability. Such a commission might also award credentials to news organizations that have earned recognition for integrity and competence—not unlike lawyers and surgeons. Ethically motivated enterprises, in a society that can and will reward excellence and honesty, may find out that doing the right thing provides greater benefits and satisfaction, than trying to "game the system."

The need for truth will grow unless we drift into barbarism. That need should become a hallmark of success in the news business—and wherever the public interest is paramount.

Reinhold Niebuhr, a distinguished theologian, wrote an essay in 1946, entitled "The Role of the Newspapers in America's Function as the Greatest World Power." He exhorted journalists to present the facts even when they ran "counter to our presuppositions." To place facts in the right setting would, he said, require "a moral and political imagination."

Due diligence and imagination do not usually sleep in the same bed, but Niebuhr realized that the press must look below the surface to find truth in public affairs where politics and morality intersect.

There is—and always has been—a symbiosis between the intellectual content of news media and the technology that permits its dissemination. The progress in paper-making, printing, broadcasting and Internet all had an effect on the content of journalism, not least the speed with which it could be conveyed. The size of circulation, the growth of advertising and the evolution of electronic communication crucially influenced style, substance and revenue. The proliferation of social media on platforms such as Facebook and Google intensified concerns over data collection and privacy. It has also brought some government intervention into what are essentially private corporate enterprises.

The large digital companies involved have not yet developed news reporting as part of their business models, and may welcome legal boundaries that are administered uniformly by the government—or some other outside organization—rather than becoming part of competitive, commercial planning. The primary interest for the platform companies has been data and advertising, which have increased exponentially over the past decade to multi-billion dollar annual levels. The production of news involves legal exposures—libel, slander, "fighting words," and other content complications. Government regulation may relieve major platforms of potential lawsuits and public relations costs regarding inappropriate material. The misuse of social media in the 2016 election is a prime example. There is, of course, the unavoidable question of how much interference an agency (such as the FCC) might inflict on corporate managements, and the technical expense of complying with regulations, whatever they may be.

Facebook and Google distribute journalism products, including social media, but they have not yet begun the production of news reporting. Facebook is currently negotiating partnerships with established news groups such as Buzzfeed and Vox, and cable news channels such as CNN and Fox. Several news programs are planned that will be seen on Facebook exclusively. What Facebook has been creating most profitably to date is the audience research that attracts large advertising contracts. The controversial privacy issues that provoked Congressional hearings in 2018 were triggered by the manipulation of private data. That problem may reappear when compiling and editing the planned news programs.

All these considerations have their roots in the evolution of news media over approximately three hundred years of American history. The political and philosophical conflicts of interest surrounding a business dedicated to both the public interest and the bottom line began long ago. To arrive at solutions for the protection of privacy, freedom of expression, and entrepreneurial ingenuity we should revisit the tumultuous history of the business. From the Zenger trial to *New York Times v. Sullivan* to *Citizens United*, the central challenges remain alive, and potentially damaging, whether in irresponsible tabloids or on the cacophonous Twitter.

Historically, violations of ethical standards were never easily defined nor adjudicated. The behavior of the press has been left to its proprietors. There were few moral equivalents in the formative early years of the Republic, and there are few in the latest digital revolution. Moral decisions inevitably involve "weighing and weighting" competing principles, and a consideration of the context in which we find ourselves. The debate over a free and independent press continues stubbornly, and there is little reason to believe that disagreements will not become a similar presence in the approaching era of "artificial intelligence." Robots might write editorials.

These essays look back at some of the seminal events, and the principal actors, in the long running, often contentious conversation carried on by America's democracy about the right to know—and the right to be wrong.

The voices are rising.

—S.E.F.

1

Oracles and Origins

MOST HISTORIANS AGREE that the actual recordings of words and data began in Mesopotamia, now southern Iraq, around 3,000 BC. Not many people could write in those times, and those who could became known professionally as scribes. This small group achieved considerable influence and power because of their verbal skill. Over time, and in different parts of the world, language evolved and spread, but the benefits of mastering its use never diminished.

Writing things down required various tools and materials. The ancient Greeks, however, began communicating with each other by telling stories which were memorized, repeated, and eventually converted to a written form by the scribes, and later on by literate monks. We should credit the ancient Greeks with inventing vowels for their alphabet, which made it possible to translate the languages of other cultures. Greek merchant ships sailing the Aegean Sea and beyond brought home news and ideas from European and African countries. It was said that the Greek traders became "intellectual burglars." They returned with the knowledge of other cultures and enlarged what they had learned. Among their adaptations were the basic principles of democracy—one man one vote; a strong middle class; and an informed electorate. The organization of government and commerce in a democracy required openness and awareness of public affairs. During the evolution of Greek democracy, the process of governing was made available to the citizens who could attend most of the meetings and debates of the governing bodies. But the distribution of information, poetry, and fiction would not be widespread until the arrival of the printing press in the 1460s. The German inventor Johann Gutenberg perfected the press by introducing movable type made of a durable alloy that could be used multiple times without loss of quality. Books and other publications soon became affordable.

Printing alarmed some scholars and religious leaders who feared the promulgation of error and blasphemy. But the desire for printed knowledge had been unleashed and the production of books and journals grew rapidly and irresistibly.

The organization of governments and commerce needed some means of informing the population, and soon the concept of news publications took root. Curiosity and need produced incentive and expansion.

Newspapers began to thrive. Urban circulations climbed and advertising revenue followed. By the end of the 19th century, publishing large circulation newspapers became a profitable enterprise. Since the earliest formation of human communities, there had been curiosity among various groups about their neighbors. When languages were developed, the curiosity could be answered. The appeal of news reporting followed in that tradition.

The early American newspapers which first appeared during the Colonial years, were as various as their owners. Some were convenient metaphorical megaphones for a given point of view, others were more high-minded than polemical. Very few dabbled in radical policy. Cumulatively the papers shared an interest in what concerned their small individual constituency—the common ground of survival, economically and politically. It was not surprising that most of the proprietors of these papers eventually embraced the need for independence from England and supported the democratic ideals of the Founders who were opposed to monarchy and formal class distinctions.

As the distribution of news developed over time it also contributed to the local economy as employer, taxpayer and marketing instrument. Newspapers were the dominant advertising platform in America for the first 150 years.

In the twentieth century, radio brought the headlines to millions of homes, but the most powerful messenger in the second half of the century was television. Video captured the largest audiences for daily news, and surveys over the last fifty years determined that more than two thirds of American adults got the preponderance of their news from television.

This exposure was augmented eventually by the cable stations with news channels operating around the clock.

In recent years the development of computer-generated news introduced the most challenging aspect of electronic information—fragmentation. Websites, blogging, and social media have created a feedbed for news reporting that often migrated to cable and then to national television networks. The online presentation of news was a natural consequence.

Contemporary newspapers have explored online publishing with some success, but revenue from advertising online—among print publications—is often below what it was during the high circulation years.

Cyberspace is a laboratory for new kinds of reporting and creative ingenuity. It has also provided new opportunities for misinformation and falsehoods. Russia appears to be the major modern practitioner of disinformation, often using social media in Europe and the United States. Disinformation was an active strategy during the Cold War. One pernicious example was the claim planted by the Soviets that AIDS was a CIA plot which somehow got out of control. Recently, a prominent Russian television personality observed that the age of neutral (fair and balanced?) journalism is over. "If we do propaganda," he said, "then you do propaganda, too."

The rise of electronic media—radio, television, and the Internet—brought governments more actively into the arena as regulators and political manipulators. In America there is the Federal Communications Commission (FCC) working on

the federal level, and the local authorities dealing with cable facilities including licenses, fees, taxes, and a certain amount of venality where corporations and officialdom intersect. The press has seldom been completely free—at least not in the constitutional sense. That reality speaks to a fundamental question among American news organizations: How do you serve the public good while seeking to make a profit?

There has always been the long shadow of dual motives in the news business—making money (at least making ends meet) while providing useful information, accurately and fairly, to a diverse electorate.

Obviously the growth of digital operations, large and small, has threatened print

> **The press has seldom been completely free—at least not in the constitutional sense.**

media economically. This has led to much venturing into online activity by print journalism companies, and entrepreneurs, with the complexity of legal rights on all sides. The *New York Times* reported that in the autumn of 2016 the *Newspaper Association of America*, which is the trade group that has spoken for major newspaper publishers since 1887, changed its name to the *News Media Alliance*—one consequence of a vastly changed news environment.

Cyberspace has accentuated the traditional media problems of privacy, misinformation, *dis*information (the deliberate distortion of information as opposed to mere error), libel, and national security. Social media seems to have no ethical boundaries. Faceless, anonymous bluster and venom appear with apparent immunity in ceaseless flow. The aspirations to provide transparency and responsibility in public affairs reporting face different problems online than those decisions once made in newspaper and television news rooms, where some thought and time could be given to a moral compass.

The political ferment of national elections has illuminated the ability of the news media to distort or reveal, confuse or explain, and on occasion inspire or motivate public opinion.

Attacks on American institutions made for politically partisan purposes risk critical damage to what has been called the *social compact*. That ideal assured a basic respect for America's core principles and the constitutional rights shared by every citizen, whatever his or her political affiliation. However, the 2016 attacks on the press threatened the "sentinel over all our liberties," in Madison's memorable words. Cynically eroding the trust between the public and the journalists who report what the government— and large corporations—are doing in the public interest

> *The political ferment of national elections has illuminated the ability of the news media to distort or reveal, confuse or explain, and on occasion inspire or motivate public opinion.*

(or against it), has weakened an essential factor in the function of democracy.

At the end of Donald Trump's first year as President, trust in the news media had fallen significantly. Nearly half the Republican voters said they did not believe the traditional media. The Trump campaign had launched an aggressive effort to brand any criticism of his views as "fake news"—a label that was repeatedly used in his Twitter messages and rare interviews. Trump's principal ally in the strident manipulation of publicity was Fox News, which defended his actions consistently.

The loss of trust and the use of carefully organized online "bots" to spread what were often intentional falsehoods succeeded in arousing doubts and skepticism, but the ease with which millions of people were persuaded to blindly accept the dismissal of traditional news, and to embrace seemingly obvious political distortions and exaggerations without evidence, was puzzling. Many theories were offered by analysts. Some attributed the development to embittered white male voters who had lost jobs and resented immigrants. Others pointed to hate groups—white supremacists, Ku Klux Klan members, neo-Nazis, and their fringe sympathizers. There was in addition always the suspicion of Russian activity. None of the explanations were able to account for the willingness of so many Americans—estimated between 30 and 40 million—to believe unproven, fictional charges against those who opposed Trump's ambitions. One incessant theme was Hillary Clinton's alleged wrongdoing, which appeared in the President's "Tweets" long after the election. Inescapably, "Tweeting" became the President's favorite method of communication.

Our children and grandchildren will be part of a prolonged and crucial struggle to find an acceptable set of rules for managing the Internet. The actions of Russian "trolls" during the

2016 campaign, the evidence that foreign agents could so easily launch millions of automated messages to targeted audiences in America, and the gathering awareness that hate merchants and extremist organizations are seeking recruits through the Internet, have alarmed both the managers and the consumers of information platforms such as Google and Facebook. What they do about such distortions—and the persistent concerns related to privacy—will determine their future.

The Internet was developed as a kind of public utility available to all on an equal basis, but the purveyors of news are private companies and they are not expected to provide hate, slander, falsehoods or foreign propaganda. The neo-Nazi websites and white supremacy publications, for instance, have recently been largely banned by the major platforms.

What they do about such distortions—and the persistent concerns related to privacy—will determine their future.

Germany has established very large fines that are imposed on companies that do not take down illicit messages, or objectionable material, within 24 hours.

The British Internet system is monitored by an independent group called the Internet Watch Foundation, which is currently funded by the communication companies and advises those same companies on what material should be blocked. It seems to be working so far on a voluntary basis. However, leaders in both the public and private sectors will have to decide how to preserve freedom of expression, privacy, and free enterprise while preventing the deliberate use of false information to manipulate public opinion. Such efforts will need the kind of good will and collaboration not easily mobilized in what many believe is becoming a "tribal" society.

To understand the dilemmas of the media, we must examine the history, the issues, and the influence of American journalism in the context of a vulnerable democracy, and a so-called "sovereign people" who need reliable information on which to base their choices—politically, socially, and morally. The early days of journalism in the colonies, and in the fledgling country called the United States, are revealing and instructive. Much has changed, but many of the philosophical and ethical debates that were born with the freedom of expression in America, remain at the center of the conversation—and the ferment—of an independent and deeply troubled press.

A free and responsible press will always be vital to the democratic process, but its dedication to principles and moral purpose are not guaranteed. The remedy of course is as it always has been—self-regulation and accountability. No other private enterprise has the Constitutional protection given to the news media, and no corporation ought to accept that protection without an obligation to serve the public interest before any private gain.

2

Reciprocity Between
the Constitution and the Press

THE COLONIAL YEARS in America were a long and troubled rehearsal for a new form of democracy called the United States.
The American form of government was considered an "experiment" by the Founders. No other nation in the history
of civilization had determined that it would start at the bottom. By giving the vote to ordinary citizens the Founders purposefully sought to create a "sovereign people." Emigrants
to America had come from countries where power always
emanated from the top—royal families, church officials, and
landowners.

To provide the information the people would need to make
their own judgments of political candidates and public policies, the Founders—without exception—endorsed a free and
independent press. The empowerment was in the text of the
First Amendment, which stated "Congress shall make no

law...abridging freedom of speech, or of the press."

It became clear that the deal a nation strikes with its press defines that nation. No government can call itself a democracy unless it has a free and independent press. Newspapers first, then the electronic press, and ultimately the Internet provide analysis and criticism of elected officials and public policy. Criticizing the government is an essential aspect of the debate and dissent that are at the core of democracy. That debate can and should be "uninhibited, robust, and wide open"—as the Supreme Court observed.

Between 1640 and 1820 there were more than 2,120 independent newspapers published in the colonial territories, and eventually the states. The largest number appeared in the middle-Atlantic states from New York to Maryland. More than half of them went out of business within two years; despite their small circulations—less than 300 copies on average—the cost of production was high and revenue was inadequate.

Newspapers were usually passed around and nearly always available in taverns, which were ubiquitous. Working men gathered at the end of each day for a drink and conversation. Settlers in a frontier land were hungry for news. Those who were illiterate—and many were in these formative years—could listen to the newspapers being read aloud in the taverns (in effect, America's first news broadcasts).

There was much interest among emigrants about what was going on in neighboring colonies. Some tavern owners subscribed to half a dozen papers and displayed them on racks near the bar. They were delivered by stagecoach and were eagerly awaited. When Ben Franklin became Deputy Postmaster General for all the colonies in 1758, he changed the rules so that all newspapers would be treated the same by the post office delivery system. For many years it cost publishers "ninepence" for each 50 miles of transport.

Franklin himself was one of the more successful publishers. His *Pennsylvania Gazette* survived for 87 years in Philadelphia. As time passed and the cities enlarged, circulations went up and advertising increased. Commenting on the early years, newspaper historian Clarence Brigham wrote:

> "Not only political history, but religious, educational and social history find place in news pages. Literature, especially essays and poetry, was constantly supplied to its readers. If all the printed sources of history for a certain century, or decade, had to be destroyed, save one, that which could be chosen with the greatest value to posterity would be a file of an important newspaper."

Brigham is writing here of an "important" newspaper. He was mindful of the border between serious, principled news reporting and the realm of tabloid news, sensationalism, and bias that has also presumed constitutional protection.

There was once no other way for Americans to find out what actions were taken by legislative bodies, or what opinions were expressed by elected officials, except by reading "important" newspapers. Only a privileged few could travel to the political meeting places, or learn what was going on first hand at the dinner tables of influential public figures.

The advent of radio and television, and the explosive growth of Internet and digital communication, have not changed the qualities of accurate, responsible journalism. It may be easier now to misinform and confuse, but truth remains demonstrable through evidence, perhaps more so with the aid of computers. Freedom of expression cannot be policed, but accountability is a requirement of credible self-regulation by the press. Over time eloquent voices in the news business have reminded fellow practitioners that the First Amendment protection carries with it a moral obligation to the readers, listeners and viewers to strive for truth telling, fairness and responsibility.

> *It may be easier now to misinform and confuse, but truth remains demonstrable through evidence, perhaps more so with the aid of computers.*

Because journalism does not have an oath of office, nor specific training requirements, there has been less institutional feeling and loyalty than a professional status might inspire. If news organizations of all kinds—print, television, digital—were to voluntarily form an independent monitoring agency with a clear mandate, there might be defined benchmarks—at least regarding accuracy, fairness, and the correction of errors. Some inside the media will believe that any criticism from the outside is interference, but the survival instinct may run deeper.

The highbrow magazines that began to appear in the 1880's persistently took up the concerns of intellectuals about the quality of journalism generally, and the role of the press in American life, which greatly enlarged during the industrial surge after the Civil War.

One of the best small publications of the time, the *Dial*, in 1893, offered a concise ethical guideline for responsible newspapers:

1. Collect news scientifically with accuracy, as the primary consideration.

2. Select and present news based on sound judgment of significance to the public, not on sensational qualities.

3. Express the views of the publication based on well-defined principles and honest convictions.

Were such simply stated ideals attainable? There were public intellectuals and a few dedicated publishers such as Charles A. Dana of the *New York Sun*, and Whitelaw Reid of the *New York Tribune* who, in large part, agreed with the *Dial*'s admonitions. Some of them were attracted to the possibility of an endowed press. They believed that the press, if supported by an endowment, would not have to bend its knee to the power of advertising—and would share the same fiduciary and ethical obligations as medicine, law and the academy. In other words, journalism could become a true profession.

Educators joined the conversation with advocacy for graduate schools, and graduate degrees in journalism, that would create a pool of intellectually (not only vocationally) trained professionals. That aspiration took some time to raise its flag, but it began to fly in the twentieth century. A moral compass for journalists was the goal.

They believed that the press, if supported by an endowment, would not have to bend its knee to the power of advertising—and would share the same fiduciary and ethical obligations as medicine, law and the academy.

Moral ambiguity remains the fashionable description of what ails the news media when it allows fact and fiction—a mixture of reality and pseudo-reality based on staged events—to commingle without a clear distinction between the two. Political events are stage-managed, especially in election years. The theatrical effect of lighting, music, and sound effects have little to do with the realities of leadership and much to do with the manipulation of voting blocs and special interest groups.

How can the press, in all its forms, separate fact from fiction? Truth, Aristotle declared long ago, is somewhere between the outer edges but not necessarily in the middle. Journalism, even at its best, seeks the truth without a basic set of rules or standard texts—and without a supervisory agency watching over its practices.

Journalism grew out of the curiosity and needs of Americans from many countries and traditions, who had settled thousands of miles away from their native societies. The old ways that were left behind included class distinction, and the surveillance by some higher authority not of public choosing. These characteristics were remembered with little affection. The hunger for freedom found its voice in the newspapers of a very young nation, well-rehearsed and confident. The Constitution provided opportunity for a free press, a curious electorate, and the moral compass they might mutually conceive.

3

The Press in the
Nineteenth Century

IN MAY OF 1787, the delegates to what was called the Federal
Convention began to arrive in Philadelphia. George Washington was soon elected as their President. Most of the delegates
agreed that their discussions should be conducted in secrecy.
Newspaper coverage was to be avoided. Washington firmly
supported the view that the presence of reporters, or any
contact with them, would discourage candid, open debate
and the possibility of changing positions—for fear of being
accused of inconsistency by the press. Thus, long before the
Constitution was drafted the influence of newspapers was
widely felt, and public opinion was respected—if not feared.

The background of the delegates was distinguished.
Among them were well known representatives such as
James Madison, George Mason, Gouverneur Morris, James
Wilson, Benjamin Franklin, and Alexander Hamilton. Roger

Sherman of Connecticut was the only delegate to have signed the Continental Association of 1774, the Declaration of Independence, the Articles of Confederation and, ultimately, the Constitution. Thomas Jefferson was in Paris during the Convention negotiating a peace treaty with the French government on behalf of a nation not yet fully formed. He did, however, converse with Madison by mail. Their letters are a revealing commentary on crafting a government.

Many early American aspirations were expressed in newspapers owned or controlled by individual politicians. Historians who wrote about the founding of the United States frequently referred to specific "gazettes"—a word used, at times, as a synonym for the press. Hamilton, for instance, gave financial support to the "*Gazette of the United States*". He expected and received a pro-Federalist (strong central government) tilt from the editor. Jefferson and Madison persuaded a New York editor to launch a pro-Republican (strong localized government) paper called the "*National Gazette,*" in Philadelphia, which was America's capitol city from 1790 to1800. Jefferson assured the editor that he would have government "advertising"—usually announcements of official rulings and regulations—placed in his paper.

During the first decades of the American Experiment, little knowledge (if any) of government (local, state, or national) would have reached the vaunted common man without the circulation of gazettes and their equivalents. The first regular newspapers in America were published in Boston in 1704 and

1719, then a paper appeared in Philadelphia, and in New York City around 1725. When Noah Webster founded his paper, "*The New York Minerva*", in 1793, he told his readers, "In no other country on earth, not even in Great Britain, are newspapers so generally circulated among the body of the people, as in America."

Many early American aspirations were expressed in newspapers owned or controlled by individual politicians.

The emerging press was irreverent, occasionally scurrilous, and preponderantly partisan, but a multitude of conflicting opinions could usually find a place among them. Somehow in the first phase of American journalism, driven by diversity and the people's appetite for news, debate and statesmanship provided most of what was wanted—even for the newborn country's leaders.

Throughout the nineteenth century, however, critical changes took place in the American newspaper business. Expanding sales numbers permitted the publishers to sell each copy for as little as a penny. Railroads were being built rapidly enough to provide wider distribution systems. The telegraph and improved printing presses could produce and deliver the news more often, and more swiftly. Meanwhile the churches and schools were teaching more people to read. News began to engage community needs—marriages, obituaries, and government notices, along with local and national politics.

In 1840 the news business was analyzed by the Federal Census for the first time. The findings determined that newspapers had joined schools, churches and libraries as an "educational" and "elevating" influence in society. The only difference between the press and the other "civilizing institutions" was that newspapers were a "private enterprise" (which, as noted earlier, came with a constitutional protection called the First Amendment).

By 1870, the printing industry was employing more than 30,000 people and generating $40 million a year—significant numbers at that time. The law required a report on newspapers and periodicals because of their relationship to "the moral, social, and intellectual condition of the people."

The smallest town in the country with a daily newspaper was Elko, Nevada—population 752. The smallest town with two daily newspapers was fabled Tombstone, Arizona—population 973. In 1881, the population of America was approximately 50 million. There were 970 daily newspapers with a combined circulation of 4.3 million. More papers were printed in early America than in England, France, or Germany.

News began to engage community needs—marriages, obituaries, and government notices, along with local and national politics.

The growth of advertising was not carefully calibrated in those days, but it could be measured by the taxes imposed on publishers. In 1867, newspapers paid $9.6 million on income. In 1880, the figure was $39.1 million.

The "penny press" was generally believed to attract lower income citizens who wanted non-partisan news (struggling farmers cared less about political wrangling than they did about the factors shaping commerce and agricultural life). Ultimately, the freedom from political obligation in the penny press taught the higher-priced "quality" papers a lesson. The quality press shifted their sensibilities towards non-partisan, i.e. *independent* journalism. Cumulatively, this development contributed significantly to the education of the reading public.

By the end of the Nineteenth Century, independent papers had become considerably better at reporting the news, and aware that their readers preferred a paper without political alliances. Independence did not mean *indifferent* or *neutral*. It did call for keeping opinions on the editorial page and assuring fair coverage of competing interests and unpopular views. Such balance was rarely achieved, not least because it was so difficult to define. How true that remains in contemporary journalism, when the country is so divided, presents a troubling issue.

The Convention delegates who had excluded the press in 1787 nevertheless voted for the Bill of Rights in 1791 with its First Amendment protection. What surprised historians was the widespread aptitude among them for *using* the press. This disposition was so common in the ranks of the "people's representatives" that the vision of a dispassionate, deliberative body shielded from special interests, and wealthy constituents, had nearly vanished by the next election. It is ironic that politicians in the earliest years of American independence gave unfettered freedom to the press and learned so quickly how to manage the influence of publicity.

George Washington, speaking to the Constitutional Convention, had asked: "If to please the people, we offer what we ourselves disapprove, how can we afterward defend our work?" He was, it would seem, thinking about those frustrated reporters waiting in the taverns near the Convention Hall.

4

―――

The Concept:
A Well-Informed Electorate

IN 1798, SEVERAL years after passing the Bill of Rights, Congress passed the Sedition Act. That statute made it a crime to publish "false, scandalous and malicious" criticism of the government, Congress, or the President. But who would decide? The Sedition Act was in the view of many an imprudent rationale for censorship of the press urged on by President John Adams, who was particularly sensitive to press criticism.

The legal content of press freedom is found in American legislative history. Because the privately owned newspapers were subject to commercial regulation like any other business, but protected from editorial interference by the First Amendment, attempts to control the press were rare but serious. The Sedition Act of 1798 passed the Senate 18-6 and the House 44-41. Editors, scientists, publishers and even a congressman were fined and imprisoned for sedition. They were all eventually pardoned by Jefferson in 1801, but never recovered their stiff fines as ordered by the pardon.

In 1815, John Adams reflected on sedition when he wrote: "If there is ever to be an amelioration of the conditions of mankind—philosophers, theologians, legislatures, politicians, and moralists will find that the regulation of the press is the most difficult, dangerous and important problem they have to solve. Mankind cannot now be governed without it, nor at present with it."

The Sedition Act was in the view of many an imprudent rationale for censorship of the press urged on by President John Adams, who was particularly sensitive to press criticism.

The Sedition Act remained in force among the separate state constitutions even though it was discredited as a federal instrument. However, because of World War I security concerns, two relevant laws were passed at the federal level—the Espionage Act in 1917 and a new Sedition Act in 1918.

The combined effect of these two statutes made it possible, for a brief period, to suppress nearly all criticism of government actions in print or speech. Approximately 2,000 individuals were prosecuted. Most of the cases concerned complaints about the war effort. More than half of those charged were found guilty. Conviction could bring as much as 20 years in prison and a $10,000 fine. Nine cases reached the Supreme Court and the government's charges were upheld in all of them. Rejection of the Sedition Act, along with a solid affirmation of the press as a watchdog over government abuse of power, did not fully materialize until 1964—more than 160 years after John Adam's presidency. Sedition charges as a means of legal repression were uncommon during that period but remained possible at the state level—hanging over the press like the Sword of Damocles.

The 1964 Supreme Court decision in *New York Times v. Sullivan* finally ensured the demise of the 1798 Sedition Act. It also set the compass for the turbulent future of free speech and press in America. The theory supported by the Court's decision was that no information which we might need to decide how to vote should be denied to the public. This did not permit, however, malicious falsehoods or reckless disregard of the facts. When these lines are crossed, and how their legal consequences are to be measured, have been part of the national conversation—and many a lawsuit—ever since.

Seemingly independent of editorial policies, technological revolutions in the communication business changed the nature of news reporting, and the national conversation about free expression. With the development of wire services such as the Associated Press (AP) and improved printing presses, newspaper circulations increased rapidly in urban areas. Radio news in the 1920s and 30s added little depth but covered the headlines and major events. The Twentieth Century would witness the contest between the power and profit of mass circulation news organizations on the one hand, and the survival of the Founder's vision of an informed electorate on the other. Television entered the competition in the second half of the century and the digital revolution exploded as the century ended.

Somehow, in the flux of invention and technical adaptability, certain basic elements of providing information endured. The philosopher Henry David Thoreau—a journalist as well— was interviewed shortly after the telegraph was invented in the 1840s. "The President of the United States," said the reporter excitedly, "sent a message to the Mayor of Baltimore in a matter of minutes." Thoreau pondered this news soberly, and then asked: "What did the President say?"

Thoreau believed that at the center of all journalism in whatever form—morally charged or harshly critical, shaped by spin or sodden with ignorance—are *words*. Words evoke ideas and ideas are what make life worthwhile. Words are also the voices of memory. They make the past available.

> *Words evoke ideas and ideas are what make life worthwhile. Words are also the voices of memory. They make the past available.*

Photographs, video, and digital images elicit powerful impressions, but without captions or narration they are incomplete, inexact, even misleading. Little has changed in this regard. Technology has altered the landscape, but the meaning of the events needs the same truth-telling analysis that has always been the responsibility of a free press. Clarity and accuracy, animated by a lively style and the vocabulary of an educated writer, have never lost value or appeal. The struggle to maintain professional quality, ethical standards, and integrity in journalism today is not much different than it was for Benjamin Franklin, a newspaper publisher and Founding Father (in that order). Regarding his role as an editor and publisher, he once wrote—perhaps in recognition of the First Amendment: "I carefully excluded all libeling and personal abuse which has of late years become so disgraceful to our country."

The world as we know it has been reported to most of us, however imperfectly, by an unfettered press. The means of doing that have

Technology has altered the landscape, but the meaning of the events needs the same truth-telling analysis that has always been the responsibility of a free press.

been transformed, but finding reliable contexts will be no easier. A nation besotted with fragments of information needs a frequent reminder of the facts to test alleged truth, to arouse moral reasoning, and to preserve its freedom.

5

The Rising Years

THE HISTORIANS AND commentators, who considered the freedom of the press as the best way of informing the electorate, differed on how wide a net should be cast. Some thought the primary concern was the forming of public policy and therefore the information published should be confined to those issues that affect how we vote. Others believed that voters must acquire, in the words of Alexander Meiklejohn, "The intelligence, integrity, sensitivity and generous devotion to the general welfare that in theory casting a vote is assumed to express"—a view of the press as the agent of public virtue.

Many public intellectuals, since the founding, have speculated about the role of a free press in America. Even though they were private ventures, the newspapers which were for two centuries the major voice that could reach the voting population collectively, left the consideration of virtue largely to the churches and the legislators. There were, however, a few individual publishers, such as Benjamin Franklin, who established the tradition of editorializing. Such commentary could be, and often was, influential and inspiring. At the very least, there was in the ruminations of proprietors and editors on public matters, during the formative years of a new nation called the United States, an awareness of higher purpose.

In the first century of United States history voting was not a meaningful gesture for most Americans. Many were not permitted to vote (women, minorities, and the impoverished to begin with) and those who did go to the polls were moved by personal concerns and local interests, and not likely to become involved in philosophical rumination—except those few with the experience and imagination that enabled them to consider the future of the nation as a whole. The great majority of voters in the early years knew very little of the world outside their small regions. What they were able to learn about other countries, more often than not, came from occasional letters printed in the local newspapers.

The availability of news from distant places—nationally and internationally—was eventually provided by what was called the wire services. Machines were placed in newsrooms that could receive, not unlike the telegraph, information from many places almost constantly. The Civil War had already stimulated the use of telegraphy to get news from remote locations transmitted to newspapers and governmental agencies. Newspapers were dependent upon the collaboration of Western Union and the Associated Press for reporting and transmission of military actions.

The device of official press releases, or "bulletins," designed to control public perception of military policy, was employed— probably for the first time—by President Lincoln's Secretary of War, Edwin Stanton. In 1864 Stanton began withholding news, arresting editors, and banning correspondents from certain war zones. General Winfield Scott took

> *The availability of news from distant places—nationally and internationally—was eventually provided by what was called the wire services.*

over the telegraph office in New York City where most accounts of military actions arrived. Secretary Stanton issued his own dispatches in the form of daily messages distributed by the wire services. These official releases were meant to set the record straight but they also served as propaganda vehicles.

The Associated Press accepted government intervention during the war years, but afterward the wire services were faced with more complicated responsibilities. News became a social institution and a cultural force in the United States, at the same time that it was becoming a commodity. American institutions and business interests needed all kinds of information promptly collected and disseminated to an expanding but scattered society. The news moved upward on a list of national priorities.

Many of the nation's educators and intellectuals viewed the press as something close to a public utility. The news organizations were expected to accomplish a far greater reach than individual editors could achieve with limited staff and tight budgets. The wire services, on the other hand, could give even the smallest papers an outpost in foreign cities, and they provided commonly shared eyewitness accounts of panoply, disasters, politics and sports, taking place in locations both foreign and domestic, that would be otherwise inaccessible to the individual newspapers. Inexorably the press as an institution gained in size, profitability and influence—politically and culturally.

News became a social institution and a cultural force in the United States, at the same time that it was becoming a commodity.

Over 200 newspapers were served by the AP in 1872. By 1880 there were 357. A contract with the wire services added greatly to the value of a news organization. Service contracts were not available unless the nearest competing member agreed. This kind of control inevitably moved the larger wire services towards monopoly. In 1874 a disgruntled reject, the *New York Graphic*, had reported that Western Union "finds in the New York Associated Press its best customer and natural ally. The success of each depends mainly upon the aid of the other. The one collects, the other transmits, the news of the world. The president of the telegraph company is a trustee of the *New York Tribune* and the publisher of the *New York Times* is a director of the telegraph company."

The power of the New York AP, as early as 1870, was enormous. It controlled transatlantic cable news, most of the key stories out of Washington, and the financial news from Wall Street.

The dispatches went to eight auxiliary AP groups in the hinter-lands. AP had, in addition, exclusive agreements with Reuters, the French Agence Havas, and the German Wolff News Agency. By 1884 a presumptuous AP executive told a Senate Committee: "We are not in the newspaper business as missionaries or philanthropies, but in pursuit of bread."

> *Many of the nation's educators and intellectuals viewed the press as something close to a public utility.*

In 1890 the AP sent out 40,000 words each day. Sports news got approximately 6,000 words each night. By 1901 publisher Whitelaw Reid was disparaging what he called "prolix" journalism—material that covered too much too thinly. Vast amounts of miscellaneous information was chattering out of the AP machines, only to land in the wastebasket. Moving into the twentieth century with the United Press (UP) as a competitor, the wire services began to hire better educated reporters and editors who delivered "breaking news," updates, and bulletins with considerable skill—a kind of communal national news experience reaching hundreds of thousands of homes at the same time, and for more than half a century it was the only game in town. In the early twentieth century one of America's leading entertainers, Will Rogers, would repeatedly say to his audiences, "All I know is just what I read in the newspapers."

Printed news was a membrane wrapped around the national economy and the political tumult that nourished a sense of nationhood. Thoughtful commentators, however, were troubled by the fragmented, undifferentiated bursts of strident news from abroad. Harvard's president James Russell Lowell complained that "the telegraph strips history of everything down to the bare facts, but it does not observe the true proportion of things." Perspectives, follow-ups, and contexts were given little time or space.

In the 1920's the teletype machine arrived and in due course "punched tape" stories were delivered in standard column width. News photos came in electronically by the mid-1930's. In the 1970's satellite transmission replaced wire services. Meanwhile television news audiences were growing rapidly.

During the early days, party politics and the selection of candidates were a preoccupation. Once that focus faded—by mutual consent of political parties and the newspapers—the editorial concern shifted to economic interests. Newspapers had become the single most important marketing device for American products by the end of the Nineteenth Century. Enter advertising revenue—large, influential, and seductive.

Advertising had been important even in the colonial period. For the small, struggling papers that rose and fell before the Revolutionary War —and for years thereafter—advertisements were business news in themselves. They let people know where limited goods and services might be found. Income, however, from ads was not great enough to keep the papers alive. Subscriptions were a vital source of support. Circulation would determine survival—and profit.

On average, with the growth of urban newspapers, 55 percent of revenues came from advertising and 45 percent from subscriptions and sales. From then on, advertisers demanded perks for their money—placement in the paper, supportive editorial material, and promotional plugs, among them.

Newspapers had become the single most important marketing device for American products by the end of the Nineteenth Century.

Ad agencies were emerging in most cities and the account managers began to look at newspapers as virtual subsidiaries. They insisted on "pleasant news" in or around their ads, and they encouraged non-journalistic gimmicks to boost circulation—contests and premiums, most notably.

Proprietors expected, and got, high margins of profit, but very few editors and reporters shared in the rewards. A free press will suffer considerable skepticism, if profit seeking overwhelms responsibility. That was the case when newspapers were at their peak, and it remained that way as television news muscled onto the national stage in the second half of the twentieth century.

The expansion of influence during the last two centuries does not in itself answer the question of whether the Fourth Estate should serve primarily to inform the public on matters relevant to policy, or to cultivate public virtue. If anything, the arrival of news in its various forms—commingled or coopted by public relations, advertising, or propaganda—makes the discussion about the role of the press more essential. The digital evolution that will dominate the next era reminds us that, by its very nature, the press has always defined its own place in our society. What has confounded and eluded the best practices of journalism is setting standards, and keeping

> *The digital evolution that will dominate the next era reminds us that, by its very nature, the press has always defined its own place in our society.*

them strong, under the lens of self-criticism and public accountability. How else can the press be trusted as both schoolroom and mediator in a turbulent world?

Deeply embedded in the evolution of the American press is the stubborn question of how a profit seeking commercial enterprise can be expected to render information on public affairs impartially, accurately and fairly. That call for ethical responsibility is an inescapable issue for the media in all its forms—old and new.

6

A Second
First Amendment

REGULATORY COMPLEXITY GREW rapidly as electronic communication metastasized. The preservation of privacy, civil
rights and freedom of expression were tested by technological advances. Legislation, regulatory agencies, and the intelligence community engaged the vast potentials of Internet
companies that controlled the flow of data, opinion, and ethical standards—among other factors.

To understand how we can deal with the approaching
storm of artificial intelligence we need to look at the history
of governance in the electronic communication sectors. The
problems of regulation when radio and television and cell
phones were the primary concerns are overwhelmed by the
so-called "World Wide Web." The public in general didn't
begin to have access to the Internet until 1989. Vermont
Governor Howard Dean in 2004 was the first politician who

organized a national campaign for a presidential nomination online. Four years later, Barack Obama succeeded in winning the White House by making the Internet a central force in fundraising and grass roots support. We have much to learn from history.

The rise of television in the second half of the twentieth century altered the nature and scope of news. The effect of visible reporting, live action events taking place in "real time"—all the compelling possibilities of immediacy—became available in a small rectangular window that seemed to offer a view, at one time or another, of everything going on in the world. Suddenly there was movement with the sound.

In the early days the moving images were black and white, often blurry, but people peered into that window long and hard. At the outset, the competition of television with words and photographs printed on paper did not strike many critics as pivotal. Could that little window ever vanquish the news magazines and newspapers which dominated the world of public information? There was not much alarm at first. The television sets were cumbersome and expensive. Programming was limited. Unsurprisingly, the familiar patterns of news didn't change right away.

But in the board rooms and executive offices, and in academic circles, speculation and research began to proliferate. In the 1950s color had been introduced. The technology was vulnerable and the cost was high. Meanwhile the business planners who looked at the potentials of television were primarily interested in entertainment. The news potential commanded less attention, but revolutions gather up all kinds of ideas. A few broadcasters were excited by the prospect of mass communication of political events, sports, and disasters. They also considered the advertising of goods and services on a scale that could change marketing forever. In California a large TV store put up a sign—"Stop staring at your radio."

The rise of television in the second half of the twentieth century altered the nature and scope of news.

Though the technical revolution moved swiftly, news was a late bloomer. Television's commercial appeal, and the regulatory measures governing it, were preshaped by the radio business. In the 1930s and 40s there had been talented reporters on radio who fought against the current of entertainment. Using the wire services, radio news informed the public on big events hours before the newspapers could produce more comprehensive accounts. During WWII, Edward R. Murrow and his colleagues had reported in depth from Europe on radio, but institutionally radio was regarded as "outside of the sphere of the press." Only decades later did National Public Radio enter the field of mass communication with broad-based independent public affairs news.

Radio producers did not think about news as a significant part of their programing, except for emergencies or local disasters, until the pre-World War II years. Because broadcast signals were few in number and looked upon as something like a public utility, there was movement in Congress to provide monitoring and set standards. The FCC was founded in 1934 on the principle that the government had a duty to promote the welfare of the community, although often at the cost of individual rights. Supreme Court Justice William Douglas observed at the time, "The central problem of the age is the scientific revolution and the wonders and the damage it

Only decades later did National Public Radio enter the field of mass communication with broad-based independent public affairs news.

brings." One of the wonders was radio—and not long thereafter, television. Regulating them, unlike the newspapers, created concentrations of power. Douglas lamented, "Where in this tightly knit regime is man to find liberty?"

In the salad days of commercial radio—before television—the proprietors were once described as "lineal descendants of operators of music halls and peep shows." It was "show biz" not "First Amendment biz." The electronic news media—radio and television—eventually settled for licensing agreements with the Federal Communication Commission in their effort to separate themselves from entertainment. The FCC, it was assumed, would be non-partisan and could not constitutionally censor content. In the Communications Act of 1934, Congress had given further protection against censorship by including provisions for appeals to Federal Courts if broadcasters felt they were unfairly regulated. On the other hand, some kind of government supervision has been part of the electronic communication ventures from the beginning—and remains so. Political interests and lobbying are inevitably involved, if not codified.

Legal scholars have debated over legislation that would separate electronic and print journalism. Some officials wanted stronger rules for radio and television; others advocated no distinctions—leaving the press in any form to the First Amendment. A third opinion wanted regulation of radio and television specifically because of scarcity and pervasiveness. Scarcity was an issue historically because of the limited number of broadcast signals. It was also widely noted that the cost of radio and television stations was so great that only corporations, or exceptionally wealthy individuals, could afford to buy them. One way or another, scarcity based on economic factors could deny dissenting views an opportunity to be heard.

> *Legal scholars have debated over legislation that would separate electronic and print journalism.*

In 1974 the Supreme Court (in *Miami Herald v. Tornillo*) found that newspapers had a constitutional right to print whatever editorial opinions they liked—despite the possibility of regional monopoly among news organizations and television networks. A prevailing view developed, however, that electronic communications were so far-reaching and instantaneous, so expensive, so mesmeric and influential that they needed at least minimal regulation. Those who supported a different restraint on the electronic press, as opposed to print, argued that the "very free" print press would itself act as a watchdog on any abuse of the regulatory power over the "nearly free" broadcast press. It was expected that traditional newspaper editorial pages would comment forcefully,

One way or another, scarcity based on economic factors could deny dissenting views an opportunity to be heard.

out of self-interest, if the government encroached on "electronic news" First Amendment rights. This was a presumption that caught on and was embraced by lawyers at cable news, satellite, and computer companies in the Brave New World of technology.

The doctrine of the FCC was allegedly "in the public interest," but what is in the public interest doesn't always interest the public. This was not troublesome in the early days of radio, but the development of networks brought concerns for local affiliates and their right to produce independent programming. The major networks—NBC, CBS, and ABC—decided to fight FCC authority. They maintained that the FCC was not in the anti-trust ballgame and had no right to interfere in the management of networks. They also claimed First Amendment rights.

In 1943 the Supreme Court had rejected most of these arguments. The Court found that the 1934 Communications Act was a proper exercise of Congressional authority over commerce. The standard for licensing a radio station was "the public interest, convenience, or necessity." It determined that such criteria were not a "denial of free speech." Radio was considered a business enterprise using public resources to provide entertainment and sell various products. Television was still off stage.

The bottom line remained scarcity. The need to allocate limited broadcast frequencies could only be addressed by the government. As for a news operation, the FCC said it must be "fair in that it accurately reflects the opposing views." The problem for many legal scholars was not "freedom to speak" by individuals in their daily lives. More important was "freedom of speech" by collectivities—political groups, constituencies, or public affairs organizations. The concern then becomes who speaks and when.

If such decisions are made by the market (profitability) there is the likelihood that some dissident voices will never be heard. The market, after all, is not unbiased. It favors commercialism and popularity—not necessarily truth or wisdom or nuance. There were (and still are) many critics who maintain that control of the market belonged to those with great wealth and large advertising budgets. Once more, only the government could create access for dissident opinions.

The bottom line remained scarcity. The need to allocate limited broadcast frequencies could only be addressed by the government.

Debate on this contention tended to favor those who controlled the market. In the late twentieth century the FCC repudiated the "Fairness Doctrine"—a policy that had required radio and television station owners to reserve airtime for outsiders to offer alternative views on public affairs issues.

By the end of the eighteenth century newspapers were relatively easy to print and individuals, or groups, seeking to speak out on public policy differences could buy into an existing paper or publish one themselves. Such a remedy was, of course, localized and reached small audiences. But it was not out of reach financially. Once mass circulation papers took over—and later radio and television networks—scarcity became the rule, not the exception, in terms of providing pluralistic public discussion.

The First Amendment forbid the Congress to write any laws *abridging* free speech or press, but it did not say the government shall take no action to enlarge that freedom, or express its own position on public policies. At least in part, this was the rationale for the founding of public radio and public television. Money collected by the state is "public money," and those who are not entirely comfortable with the market as the dominant force in First Amendment policies, believe state revenues can be constitutionally used to preserve democracy by making sure differing views on public matters are heard.

In 1969 the Supreme Court had upheld the idea of a "new" First Amendment—"One befitting the 'new' method of communication." However, this interpretation does not offer quite the same Constitutional protections for television news that are available to print news. The Court's assumption was that "entertainment" is not a contributor to the "public debate" sheltered by the First Amendment. Television was thought to be primarily entertainment, as radio had been—even in the interpretation of the "new" First Amendment and the licensing of corporate facilities.

Serious television newscasts finally began in the mid-twentieth century as 15-minute programs largely devoted to the reading on camera of wire service news material. When newscasts expanded a few years later to a half hour, the pattern became 22 minutes of news and 8 minutes of commercials, promotions, titles, credits and so on. Over time the audience grew and so

> *The Court's assumption was that "entertainment" is not a contributor to the "public debate" sheltered by the First Amendment.*

did news aspirations and revenue. The newscast "anchors" became familiar figures who had ingratiating personalities and prestige, which seemed to inspire public trust. We are reminded that in the closing years of the twentieth century nearly two-thirds of the American adult population received most of their news from television.

Despite its reach and its proliferation the most influential argument for regulating electronic news remains scarcity. Too many people still want broadcasting licenses and the government still has only a few to give away. The Supreme Court accepted the scarcity rationale, but cable television arrived as a horse of a different color. Congress passed the Cable Communication Act in 1984, which gave municipalities a certain number of local access channels for public *and* private purposes.

Because of First Amendment challenges such as hate speech, indecency, and political slander, cable confronts

We are reminded that in the closing years of the twentieth century nearly two-thirds of the American adult population received most of their news from television.

some content regulation at the federal level, and franchise (commercial) regulations at the local level. Video "streaming," conveyed by the Internet, is subject to similar controls not yet fully defined.

When a cable company seeks First Amendment constitutional rights, the courts have to examine several difficult questions. First, is there any point in continuing to call cable a scarcity when by its very nature—and certainly by utilizing the Internet—there is abundance? Second, is there a convincing argument that the cost of creating and running a cable company amounts to "economic scarcity" (which is to say, only a few can afford the gamble)? Third, is each cable company a virtual monopoly because only one of them can survive in each community, and consequently only one is given a franchise? This kind of monopoly automatically invites regulation. And finally, there is the constitutionality of enforcing public access. The government cannot force a newspaper to publish an op-ed page. Why should it have the right to force a cable operator to produce the electronic equivalent of an op-ed page? Can cable be characterized as a public utility, a kind of "common carrier" like transportation? All these complex questions endure.

The government as a regulator (i.e., the FCC, whose members, we should be aware, are appointed by the President), and the private corporations as selectors of news (TV networks, newspaper companies) are presumably serving the public interest. However, they also have the power to manipulate or censor the product. If the media are controlled by the market (advertising and circulation revenue), what is the countervailing power that can protect the public interest?

One segment of opinion among scholars and commentators insists that the government (again) is the only authority that can make sure those issues, often neglected or distorted systematically, receive a place on the public agenda. How else to assure legitimate viewpoints are heard that are otherwise almost left in silence?

Predictably, there is a segment that sees the *press* as the countervailing power to the government. The relationship between government and the free press has been likened to the confrontation of the prosecutor and the defense in a courtroom. Some people believe that the market can have a distorting influence on both politicians and the press. A second group of analysts sees what law professor Alexander Bickel called a necessary "contest between press and government because in it lies the optimal assurance of both privacy and freedom of information. Not full assurance of either, but maximum assurance of both."

The most troubling question posed by the current growth of digital versatility is how to shape our future as a decent, viable society. Education is the savior, curator and designer of the future. Out of vast expansion of technology, and the immeasurable flow of data, hard choices must be made. They will require a well-informed understanding of evidence if we are to produce sensible guidelines for human society in a world of artificial intelligence and robotics. Data, our scientists tell us, is the coin of the technological future, and it will, if properly analyzed, provide predictive knowledge and discovery.

The relationship between government and the free press has been likened to the confrontation of the prosecutor and the defense in a courtroom.

There are, of course, other questions. How do we protect information from unethical competition, misuse and deception? Can education produce the perceptions of principled judgment based on truth and compassion? Can education train sufficient numbers of responsible talented citizens? Will the leaders of our institutions be selected wisely? How will security be provided for the difficult transition from a chaotic 21st Century to an anticipated 22nd Century of scientific balance between human fallibility and efficient—even autonomous—machines capable of doing most of the tasks now performed by humanity, more swiftly and dependably? All these issues emanate from the technological revolution.

It is clear that the machines of the future will be born and nourished by human minds, but the advance of science suggests the machines will, in the coming decades, become virtually independent and functionally superior to their inventors. Can we educate ourselves and our "learning" machines to live together and work together in creating a new and better world? If so, we had better get started soon.

Somewhere between these concepts—and not necessarily in the middle—there is a balance that can be reliable and fair. Finding it requires a continuous process voluntarily entered into by those who care—in the media, in the government and in the electorate. The authors of the First Amendment did not say it would be easy.

7

Finding a Moral Compass

EVERY CONSTRUCTIVE HUMAN enterprise, however small or modest, needs the support of ethical standards. Human beings inevitably develop different perspectives. If they are going to work together they will have to establish some kind of rules and structures. Ethical principles, as building blocks, are the most enduring and reliable but they evolve out of experience and they are not always evident. They must frequently be excavated through provocation or rational analysis.

Individualism, and our desire for identity, are not achieved in isolation. We define ourselves in our relation to others—and to a social system of some sort. It has been said that morality is how we behave in that system, and ethics are the deep-running principles which inform our behavior. The values and goals of various social groups compete, like so many other aspects of democratic life, in the marketplace of ideas. People must choose between ultimate values, and such choices would be more wisely made if they were based on presumed truths, ethically grounded.

Values emerge from the clash of ideas. No public figure spoke more eloquently for debate and dissent than the English political philosopher John Stuart Mill. Published in 1859, his essay "On Liberty" has been at the center of discussion on the moral compass ever since. Mill was a "utilitarian": His moral compass pointed to the "greatest good for the greatest number." His philosophy was a model the media could and often does adapt. He also believed profoundly in individual liberty, declaring that as long as we do no harm to others, over our own body and mind we are sovereign.

For the news media, editorial choices must be made that are not necessarily the same calculations individuals might make. Serving the "greatest number" always risks hurting the minority—the tyranny of the many over the few, or the lone dissenter. One man's meat can always be another man's poison. But making moral and intellectual choices is what distinguishes human beings from animals. Mark Twain added that only human beings can blush—which is another way of describing the moral compass. The process of arriving at enduring moral judgments can be difficult; good will and the capacity for change are required. No institution has a greater obligation—and perhaps a more conflicted task—in establishing a moral compass than the press.

The Founders gave the press its protection because they believed the citizens who elect their representatives would need adequate information about public affairs, and the candidates' qualifications for public office. Only a free and independent press can provide the necessary information and report the contrasting views of those seeking election.

The Bill of Rights recognizes the fact that governments and corporations in America cannot credibly evaluate their own actions

Mark Twain added that only human beings can blush— which is another way of describing the moral compass.

for the public. The men who composed the Constitution and wrote the Bill of Rights advocated an unfettered press, but offered no recommendations regarding responsible behavior by publishers, editors, and reporters. Nor did they anticipate the profitability of newspapers. They simply forbid Congress to pass any laws "abridging freedom of speech or of the press."

It is clear, reading their correspondence, that the Framers were aware of the influence the press would have because they had experienced it in the colonial years—the "Great Rehearsal" for independence. At least in theory, the people would be sovereign—each citizen with one vote. The process was then—and has been ever since—imperfect. In the beginning women, people of color, and those who owned no property, were denied the vote. Obviously, the most extreme denial was slavery, which in its time was a blatantly widespread contradiction of the Declaration of Independence and the principles of democracy. For some states slavery seemed to be an economic necessity, but it was a cruel exploitation of human captives wherever it existed—and surely a violation of the moral compass. It was also an inescapable stain on the Constitution.

The press was involved at every level of the slave trade. Newspapers published news of slave ships arriving at American ports, and the rewards offered for returning any slaves who managed to escape. Abolition newspapers were seized at southern post offices and destroyed. Editorials defending slavery appeared during the run-up to the Civil War. Newspapers produced disturbing stories about slavery that divided a young nation and aroused outrage on both sides. The deepest irony had festered in Virginia where the most eloquent and prominent voices for liberty and independence—Washington, Jefferson and Madison among them—were slave owners.

The moral compass in early American public life found few steady hands, but those who spoke out against slavery needed newspapers to amplify their message. Some anti-slavery publishers were attacked by mobs, their printing equipment set ablaze. Others lost their lives. The Civil War took more than 600,000 lives in all—often pitting members of the same family against

> *The deepest irony had festered in Virginia where the most eloquent and prominent voices for liberty and independence—Washington, Jefferson and Madison among them—were slave owners.*

each other. The moral issues seem in retrospect to be unavoidable and yet, at the time, pro-slavery groups believed the Bible was on their side, convincing themselves that scripture allowed slavery for the alleged inferior black race.

The press in the nineteenth century reflected bitterly opposing views and frequently supported extreme positions. A moral reckoning was seldom a priority. It was not until the twentieth century that morality became a significant concern of central figures in the press. Commentators were warning that the public would not defend the press against government supervision unless reforms were put in place. Casual invasion of privacy and the low level of moral perception were cited. Many critics blamed advertising, and the revenue it provided, for pushing newspapers into conformity, false reporting and sensationalism.

Publishers Joseph Pulitzer and William Randolph Hearst had feuded for years in what became a newspaper war in New York City during the first part of the twentieth century. Pulitzer, weary of the battle and increasingly aware of the wasted time and resources, withdrew from the contest and shifted dramatically from tabloid excesses to serious reporting based on ethical principles. He was determined to keep opinions on the editorial page, eschew gossip and scandal, and emphasize truth telling and accuracy and fairness. Such ambitions were transformational. The Pulitzer Prize that he initiated and his funding of the Columbia Journalism School were emblematic of his commitment and that of his son, Ralph, who succeeded him. That commitment helped to launch the concept of "objective journalism"— an endeavor that failed to become systemic, but opened the door to a moral compass in media newsrooms.

An eloquent advocate of objective journalism, Walter Lippmann, became the most influential analyst of the press and its role in society in the twentieth century. He was also a brilliant columnist and editor who helped start the magazine *New Republic*. In several provocative books he examined the crucial importance of the press to what was a fundamental principle of democracy—the consent of the governed. "If there is no steady supply of trustworthy and reliable news," he wrote in *Liberty and the News*, "incompetence and aimlessness, corruption and disloyalty, panic and ultimate disaster must come to any people which is denied an assured access to the facts." For Lippmann access to information, as well as the consent of the governed, were conditions cultivated by the press and necessary for a moral compass.

Lippmann saw the press as a teacher. The most formidable enemy in his intellectual universe was ignorance. Freedom, liberty and democracy, he believed, were defined and sustained by a well-informed and consenting citizenry. He wrote, sometimes in theological language, of the "truly sacred and priestly offices in a democracy, the careful, accurate ordering of news." Only independently gathered and factual information could serve the public interest. For that task Lippmann urged the recruitment of the brightest and the best people. His ideal was intelligent, motivated journalists pursuing truth with scientific thoroughness. He advocated the use of experts—especially political scientists—to help reporters and editors produce understandable accounts of complex views and positions on public affairs.

His philosophical insights did not neglect the practicalities. He recommended by-lines and mastheads so that the public would know who was responsible for what they were reading. He favored corrections and retractions of errors, and he suggested open forums

For Lippmann access to information, as well as the consent of the governed, were conditions cultivated by the press and necessary for a moral compass.

where readers could question editors and reporters on the selection of facts—the gatekeeping function, what gets into the paper and what doesn't.

A moral compass involved the creation of reliable reporting to serve a common good. In the world of news reporting, even as it migrates towards digital formats, social media, and fragmentation, Lippmann's principles have not weakened.

Unfortunately, the internal institution called the newsroom is vanishing. It was the place where a moral compass could operate, where discussion, debate, consensus and decisions on right and wrong, good and bad, truth and falseness, could be given consideration thoughtfully and collectively. The newsroom could filter the analysis of public opinion among experienced reporters and editors. It was also a place where reporters might bear witness—or, of course, stay silent for fear of job security. Following the moral compass requires courage, and, as with all truth seeking, must be wary of special interests. It should reveal the sins of commission (i.e. bias, fabrication, venality), as well as the sins of omission (i.e. self-censorship, neglected facts, dishonesty).

More subtle and frustrating for the moral compass to deal with is the loss of attention, exploration, and contemplation in the journalistic process. Digital tools, according to extensive research, can reduce our capacity to read widely and deeply. Some surveys, conducted over decades among diverse groups (including prominent academics), found that participants who were immersed in digital media for years could no longer easily read books or lengthy reports. They needed the speed and compression of computers. The learning process was central to these research projects. Is there a new kind of learning? Does the computer provide a short-cut to conclusions that were once the nuanced knowledge emerging from deep reading and deep reasoning?

For journalism, and the knowledge needed to understand public affairs, the issue could be time itself. News reporting has been called "history on the run." It asserts the presumptions of history before all the facts are in. Mill, in his historic 1859 essay noted earlier, says that the truth is never final. That same year, interestingly enough, Charles Darwin wrote *On the Origin of the Species* and Karl Marx wrote *The Critique of Political Economy*. Both works provided much controversy about the definition of truth. Mill's position was that no approximation of truth could be realized without freedom of expression— particularly dissenting views, unpopular ideas, and the most eccentric or revolutionary notions. He rejected "the deep slumber of decided opinion." His critics charged he left too many large questions unsettled. He claimed all views should be heard and debated, because presumed truth must be constantly disputed—perhaps enlarged or corrected. Disputation, Mill insisted, conducted with civility, might reveal inaccuracy on one hand, or validate the given proposition on the

For journalism, and the knowledge needed to understand public affairs, the issue could be time itself. News reporting has been called "history on the run."

other. It may be that the digital tools of modern communication will enhance that effort, but the debate continues regarding our dependence on technology. Some fear—not without evidence—that we may become "tools of our tools."

As to journalism's need for a moral compass in the transition from print to video and computer, it is essential for three reasons. First, to illuminate the political landscape; second, to permit the examination of diverse ideas in the search for truth; and third, to encourage public discussion which is necessary to a free society—and freedom of expression which is necessary to public discussion.

The two words "moral compass" can speak for themselves. The first word suggests values—the difference between good and evil, virtue and vice. The second word suggests direction and journey, the movement and the route to wise and just behavior. It is an evolving process and surely among its major narrators must be a free and responsible press.

8

The Paradox of
Self-Regulation

FROM THE EARLIEST appearance of newspapers in America during the late 17th century, nearly a hundred years before the Declaration of Independence, publishers confronted the need for ethical responsibility. Throughout the colonial era they were concerned with the attitude of governors sent from England and the possible severe penalties for sedition. Colonial governments representing the British crown were not despotic as a rule, but they could strictly enforce the laws put in place by Parliament even though the English settlers in America had no voice in that process. Criticism of officials by the American newspapers in the 16th and 17th centuries almost inevitably was characterized as sedition.

Self-regulation could become self-censorship. The alternative was a set of written ethical principles, or an independent advisory board. The nature of self-regulation by the press consequently began in the New World as a political balancing act motivated by fear. Pseudonyms were commonly employed by writers who did not want to see the sheriff at their door. Colonial jail cells were notoriously dangerous places. Barely enough food and rampant respiratory diseases were well-known hardships, but incarceration itself was so hard to survive that offenders went to great lengths to keep their identities hidden. The pseudonym device was widely utilized during the Revolution, the Constitutional Convention, and in the public arguments about slavery.

Writing in a Boston newspaper shortly before the revolution, Joseph Greenleaf—calling himself "Mutius Scaevola"—declared it would be a good idea "that the pretended governors were dismissed and punished as usurpers, and that the council, according to charter, should take upon themselves the government of the province." Similar sentiments were appearing in many colonial papers. The independence movement in America fed on such editorials.

The pseudonym device was widely utilized during the Revolution, the Constitutional Convention, and in the public arguments about slavery.

Self-regulation by the press, in more ways than one, was the aspiration.

The obligation to maintain editorial standards began with the unique exemption given by the First Amendment. Its influence in editorial decision making was perplexing on a scale not quite anticipated by the Framers, though it was somehow discernible in their philosophical writings, as it has been in the premonitions of modern commentators and the Supreme Court. Constitutional Scholar Zechariah Chafee observed that the First Amendment "protects two kinds of interests in speech...individual interests, the need of many men to express their opinions on matters vital to them if life is to be worth living...and a social interest in the attainment of truth so that the country may not only adopt the wisest course of action but carry it out in the wisest way."

The dilemmas of journalistic integrity have been examined in America for well over 200 years in numerous contexts, by many participants—newspaper editors, pamphleteers, religious leaders, foreign scholars, critics of every kind, and politicians. It was the backdrop to all partisan issues and resonated in each new election, economic crisis and moral issue. Ethical restraints slowly, cautiously entered the newsrooms and boardrooms of the mass circulation media in the 19th and 20th centuries, and eventually among the electronic tributaries such as radio and television. More recently ethics has engaged the Internet along with the major platforms, particularly Facebook and Google.

Over time the proliferation of free expression in the American press triggered the hiring of minority reporters, women, and young people seemingly attuned to dynamic new forms of journalism. They brought with them the problems of inclusiveness and the mystifications of "multi-culturalism," "political correctness" and "inequality." The contradictions were addressed in the large media organizations that affected public opinion; they are now being addressed in the scattered multiplicity of the online publishers and "social media."

How does constitutional self-regulation cross these borders? The answer—if there is one—began to form itself early in the development of the American culture, but aroused the interest of critics and commentators more urgently in the late 19th and 20th centuries.

Over time the proliferation of free expression in the American press triggered the hiring of minority reporters, women, and young people seemingly attuned to dynamic new forms of journalism.

James Madison, who contributed profoundly to the Framers' discussions of individual and civil rights, began the dialogue on the press when he famously wrote, "A popular government without popular information, or the means of acquiring it, is but a Prologue to a Farce or a Tragedy; or perhaps both. Knowledge will forever govern ignorance, and a people who mean to be their own Governors must arm themselves with the power which knowledge gives."

A fellow Virginian, Edmund Randolph, seemed to shift the burden of responsibility more directly onto the press when he lamented in a newspaper called *The Virginia Independent Chronicle*, in 1789: "The liberty of the press is indeed a blessing which ought not to be surrendered but with blood; and yet it is not an ill-founded expectation in those who deserve well of their country, that they should be assailed by an enemy in disguise, and have their characters deeply wounded, before they can prepare for defense."

The words of Madison and Randolph unknowingly set the terms for the debate regarding self-regulation by those publishers and journalists who would be given the First Amendment in 1791. Inherently the Founders had accepted that there was no way the press could be supervised or policed without diminishing its freedom. Jefferson, among many other leaders, believed unfettered freedom should be allowed in *advance* of publication, but when libelous or false information is published, the existing relevant laws should be invoked. It was this position that survived controversy and debate for nearly 200 years and finally won Supreme Court affirmation in the Pentagon Papers case of 1971—that the press should be free of any *prior restraints*, but not be above the law.

Because no prior restraints were allowed by the Constitution—in other words, no censorship—the need for self-regulation became a concern among proprietors and politicians (who were often one and the same), but an organized effort to establish suitable guidelines took many years to develop and has not yet been completed.

In reality the temptation of what Madison had called "licentiousness" was too often more appealing in the newspaper world than the exercise of self-restraint. There was always doubt about the motivations of newspaper proprietors. In 1913 alone, 20 states considered some form of newspaper regulation. Apprehensions centered around four issues: carelessness and inaccuracy; suppressing information to protect special interests; conspiring with advertisers; and the excesses of sensationalism.

Legislative remedies, however, were bound to fail for two reasons—constitutional protection and the general belief among the people in keeping the press independent. Of equal importance was the less visible effort of the proprietors to defend their turf and their profits from "outside interference."

There were other reactions to the threat of "interference," including endowment (as already mentioned). Building an endowment system for the press has been an idea floating in the background for a long time. Serious consideration by the press of endowments, funded and nourished by the country's major foundations, and private donors, seemed possible when the great philanthropist Andrew Carnegie announced his support for the concept in 1912. But the idea never attracted a strong constituency. The goal was to reduce—or eliminate—the need for advertising and the effect it had on editorial choices. The failure to

> *Apprehensions centered around four issues: carelessness and inaccuracy; suppressing information to protect special interests; conspiring with advertisers; and the excesses of sensationalism.*

achieve a commitment for endowments dampened American interest in several European experiments with tax breaks for news organizations that reduced space given to advertising, and enlarged space for news coverage. Germany and Sweden have notably legislated in favor of such experiments, which have had positive results.

The Kansas State Press Association issued the first known journalism code of ethics in 1910. That same year Professor James Melvin Lee of NYU Journalism School spoke out in favor of written codes to include monitoring of circulation claims, and the prohibition of fraudulent advertising. He was joined by the editor of the *New York Post* who concluded that "no achievement of huge circulations can compensate for the lack or loss of public respect."

The issues, and the sporadically proposed ethical standards, remained similar throughout the 18th century and into the mid-20th. The arrival of radio and television did not significantly moderate the conflict between profit and public service, though they enlarged the size of audiences and financial needs. The FCC licensing and regulatory power put electronic news under scrutiny not suffered by the printed press, but the number of licenses lost because of government regulatory action was very, very small. And so it has remained for more than a century.

One issue that affected both print and the expanding influence of television was the right to privacy. It is not mentioned in the Constitution, nor in the Bill of Rights. The idea of privacy and its place in public affairs seemed to find a small niche in the annals of legal history because of an article published in the *Harvard Law Review* in 1890. It was written by two lawyers—Samuel Warren and Louis D. Brandeis (before he became a much esteemed member of the Supreme Court). They wrote persuasively about the paucity of "propriety and decency" in the nation's press, and suggested that the laws of the land must include the protection of "the right to privacy."

One issue that affected both print and the expanding influence of television was the right to privacy. It is not mentioned in the Constitution, nor in the Bill of Rights.

Their essay noted that humankind "under the refining influence of culture, has become more sensitive to publicity, so that solitude and privacy have become more essential to the individual."

Respect for privacy became one of the many virtues responsible papers expected in their newsrooms.

In addition to this respect, the belief in public service, along with some measure of self-recognition, were reasonable aspects of loyalty to the job. Journalists could not be expected to take a vow of poverty nor would they come to think of the news business as a monastic calling. There were many ironies and hypocrisies when moral consciousness engaged the profitable power of the press. Two lessons were learned by those who seriously considered the paradox of self-regulation. First—shame and embarrassment do not enter our minds as invited guests. Second—in the words of George Bernard Shaw—"Virtue is an insufficient temptation."

9

The Pursuit of Ethics

INSTITUTIONAL CHANGE, OR reform, is almost always opposed by those who want to keep things as they are. The status quo does not depart gladly. This was the case in the ranks of America's news organizations which prospered and grew in the twentieth century. They had introduced and allowed practices as journalists and corporations that aroused public dismay, particularly among intellectuals and moralists. The philosophical basis for a free and independent press in a democracy had been corrupted by the commercialization, fabrication, and partisanship of newspapers and magazines presumably operating in the public interest. This condition troubled many distinguished commentators and some proprietors who took their obligations to the First Amendment seriously.

One of them was a very successful publisher named Henry Robinson Luce. He was born in China, where his parents were Protestant missionaries, and he lived there until he was 14.

Later he went to Yale University where he became interested in journalism. While in college, he began thinking about a business that would provide news, along with well informed opinions, in the form of a weekly magazine which permitted research and depth not possible in a daily newspaper. Luce and a college friend named Britton Hadden committed themselves to this concept, and not long after they graduated they co-founded, in 1923, *Time* magazine. It was financed by prominent figures in the business world, and it attracted readers quickly. *Time* became within a few years one of the most influential and respected news publications in the country. Its success spawned *Fortune*, *LIFE*, *Sports Illustrated* and *People* over the next half century.

Luce hired bright young men and women who were generalists. Intelligence, a good college education, and perhaps a stint at the undergraduate newspaper were the attributes he preferred. Recruits would learn their craft on the job from experienced staff, not from journalism schools which he regarded as vocational.

Luce believed that the twentieth century would be "the American Century"—a conviction he proclaimed in his own writing and in the professional environment he established at Time, Inc. The ethical context of a career at his company included a genuine separation of the business and editorial staffs. At corporate headquarters in New York, reporters and editors occupied certain floors, advertising and promotion employees other floors. They were encouraged to avoid intermingling. In principle—and in fact—the interests of advertisers were to have no influence on editorial decisions. Such precautions had not been a common occurrence in the media world, nor had an approach to news reporting that advocated the concept of integrated editorial opinions. Luce brought to journalism the moral awareness of a missionary family and the sophisticated ambitions of an entrepreneur. The co-existence of such contrasting qualities had produced many of the problems of a growing American press. The interest of spiritual leaders and those of competitive capitalists do not naturally migrate to the same table.

> *Luce believed that the twentieth century would be "the American Century"—a conviction he proclaimed in his own writing and in the professional environment he established at Time, Inc.*

It seemed to Henry Luce that it was high time the leading media companies reviewed the events and actions that had steadily lowered their reputations in the opinion polls. He wanted to see a careful, independent evaluation of the media that would recast the vital importance of a free press in a democracy. Surprisingly, he asked Robert Hutchins, former president of the University of Chicago, to chair a commission on the freedom of the press. He donated $200,000 from Time Inc. to fund the work. The appointment of Hutchins was a surprise to many because those who were familiar with Luce's views did not think the two men shared the same philosophy on public affairs or political leadership. That both men had agreed to undertake the task was, for those who knew them, a tribute to their dispassionate mutual respect.

Luce declared he would not meddle in any way. He agreed to keep hands off. He would wait for an invitation to speak (only once) to the group of intellectual paladins Hutchins had assembled, and then keep his distance. During his singular meeting with the commissioners, Luce described his sense of their investigation. He said, "It is important to produce a broader understanding in the democratic society as to the agreed standards and the responsibilities of the press."

Luce declined to suggest any specific agenda and expressed his confidence in the commissioner's diligence, but he reminded them that "You can't talk about freedom without postulating a theory of responsibility." It might be reasonable to surmise that the decision Luce made to ask Hutchins to conduct a study of the press was not unrelated to the fact that the quest for truth in journalism parallels the same quest at the center of great universities.

> *Luce declined to suggest any specific agenda and expressed his confidence in the commissioner's diligence, but he reminded them that "You can't talk about freedom without postulating a theory of responsibility."*

In the opening paragraph of the final report produced by the Commission, Hutchins did not reveal his feelings. He wrote: "In December, 1942, Henry R. Luce of Time Inc. suggested to me an inquiry into the present state and future prospects of the freedom of the press. A year later this

Commission, whose members were selected by me, began its deliberations."

The twelve members of the Commission* were mostly well known professors from major universities along with a distinguished poet and playwright (Archibald MacLeish), the Chairman of the Federal Reserve Bank of New York (Beardsley Ruml), a much esteemed theologian (Reinhold Niebuhr), and a college president (George Shuster)—all scholarly men, but no women and no black or Hispanic Americans. They met frequently from 1943 to 1946 in full session or smaller committees. They talked in depth with 58 accomplished men and women connected with news organizations (print, radio, and film). The staff of four—including one woman—recorded interviews with 225 representatives of industry, government and private groups concerned with the press. Finally, the commissioners held 17 two or three day conferences among themselves, and reviewed 176 documents prepared by the staff or individual commissioners.

Hutchins suggested they confine their report "to the role of the agencies of mass communication in the education of people in public affairs." He also insisted that every commissioner would sign off on the final text.

Hutchins was the writer who put the pieces together. He

---

* Vice Chairman Zechariah Chafee Jr. (Harvard) John W. Clark, (Columbia);
John Dickinson (Pennsylvania); William E Hocking (Harvard), Harold D Laswell
(Yale), Charles E Merriam (Chicago), Robert Redfield (Chicago), Arthur M
Schlesinger (Harvard).

observed in his introduction that had each one of the commissioners been allowed to offer his own version of specific issues regarding an ethical audit of the press at that time, the contents would have been far different. What was published reflected their shared consensus. Six "special studies" by individual commissioners and staff were also published.

The discussions, the search, and analysis took place during the war years, for the most part, and one critique many years later of the 1947 report described it in the prestigious *Columbia Journalism Review* as "in a sense a post war charter for the press." Hutchins himself acknowledged the limitations which resonate in every effort that has been made—before and since—to conceive an acceptable method for persuading the press to voluntarily abide by defined standards of ethical self-regulation. He wrote with characteristic candor: "The Commission's recommendations are not startling. The most surprising thing about them is that nothing more surprising could be proposed. The Commission finds that these things are all that properly can be done and that the neglect of them, which now imperils the freedom of the press, should be replaced by a serious and continuing concern for the moral relation of the press to society."

Hutchins suggested they confine their report "to the role of the agencies of mass communication in the education of people in public affairs." He also insisted that every commissioner would sign off on the final text.

Somewhat unexpectedly there was a chill in the air the

moment the report went public. Henry Luce made no official comment but there were many of his associates who said he was disappointed. Some critics found it too tepid. Others thought it was tilted to the left. There was a notable paucity of reporting on its content—pro or con—in the nation's newspapers. For more than 70 years historians and journalism scholars have tried to explain why.

The language of the report is scholarly, a bit legalistic (Hutchins had, after all, been the Dean of Yale Law School when he was 28 years old), philosophical and vested in the historical record. The Commission for a Free and Responsible Press had identified three fundamental reasons why the press was in trouble. First, the press was essential in a democracy and becoming more important over time, but access was decreasing for those who were not in the mainstream. Second, those who owned and controlled mass communication companies were not adequately serving the public interest. Third, in their use of the facilities (print, radio, film) the owners had produced many kinds of distorted journalism which "the society condemns." The people, the Commission warned, would take steps—politically or legally—to obtain some measure of control if changes were not made by the press establishment.

The Commission also attributed the vulnerability of a free press to profit-seeking economics, and the failure of proprietors to understand the role of the press and its responsibilities. A responsible press, the Commission declared, must be accountable to its audience.

The findings and declarations made by the Commission were placed in the framework of five standards of performance they believed were required of a "free and responsible press":

1. Provide a "truthful, comprehensive account of the day's events in a context which gives them meaning."

2. Serve as a "forum for the exchange of comment and criticism."

3. Offer a "representative picture of the constituent groups of society."

4. Present and clarify "the goals and values of society."

5. Provide "full access to the day's intelligence."

Looking back to the *Dial* Magazine in 1893, similar resolutions were not written in the context of advanced technology, but shared the same enduring perceptions of accuracy, fairness and relevance. Translating such values into day to day professionalism remains a dilemma of choices.

The suggested requirements amounted to a utilitarian ideal—the best service for the most people. They had been adapted from ideas submitted to the Commission by high level media managers from all over America. They also represented an ideal that the Commission allowed was not achievable by any one news organization, but as a cumulative aspiration for the institutional press, the five requirements became the most enduring legacy of the Commission's extensive study.

The reactions that all of these pronouncements received, however, had little to do with substance. The fear of government intervention was the central basis for resistance and the virtual silence among the major news organizations. There were many related reasons why press industry owners and managers neglected the recommendations of the Commission. Among them was the Commission's admonition that the press must remember that its moral right will be conditioned on its acceptance of accountability. This sounded to owners and managers

The suggested requirements amounted to a utilitarian ideal— the best service for the most people. They had been adapted from ideas submitted to the Commission by high level media managers from all over America.

like government interference, particularly when the text explicitly declared: "Its legal right will stand unaltered as its moral duty is performed." The public meanwhile heard or saw very little news, if any, about the Commission's views on accountability.

When the report was published in 1947, under the title *A Free and Responsible Press*, an advance press release revealed enough of the contents to make media executives very uneasy. Even though the commissioners had concluded that government was not the remedy, a great many editors were convinced that the report would lead to a monitoring body of some sort that would be a precursor to regulation. Before the document was available and its contents examined, the media was mobilizing opposition. The report had been addressed to proprietors and managers, not the working editors and reporters. Chairman Hutchins had publicly emphasized the Commission's belief in private ownership but many short-falls were identified—including more rigorous self-criticism, attention to race relations, and reporting on global issues. The primary factors that prevented professionalism, the commissioners decided, were the lack of defined standards and the ability to enforce them.

> **The primary factors that prevented professionalism, the commissioners decided, were the lack of defined standards and the ability to enforce them.**

The targeted audience was not enchanted by such commentary. They were also irritated by the *omission* of references to existing ethical codes, and alleged dedication to accuracy. Criticisms and objections were plentiful after the report was released, but praise was rare and feeble. Aside from the fear of government intervention, or oversight by so-called independent monitoring organizations, there were charges of left wing inclination and potential censorship. What it all came to, in effect, was a rejection of the Commission's thoughtful conclusions, carefully rendered after several years of listening, reading and discussion. Nothing quite like it has been undertaken since, nor has any selected group of such eminence and qualification devoted so much time and effort to an analysis of a free press.

Responsibility is the central theme. The Hutchins Commission—as it came to be known—dwelt on *social responsibility* and provided a provocative examination of its meaning. Without responsibilities to the public interest, the press becomes merely another business with no greater right to a Constitutional protection than the maker of sausages.

Despite its harsh reception the report has been a frequent subject of debate and study in journalism schools and media conferences for many decades. It began as a consideration of "the moral relation of the press to society," and it endures as a compelling contemplation of social obligations.

The report has often been cited as the most important statement on the media in the twentieth century. It did not attempt to answer specific questions that arise in the daily work of reporters and editors. Its agenda was to define the role of the press as an institution, and the appropriate function of the government and the law as guarantors of the freedom given to the press by the Constitution.

What remains to be done after these many years—and technological advances—is to establish the framework of ethical principles that will shape and encourage ethical

> *It began as a consideration of "the moral relation of the press to society," and it endures as a compelling contemplation of social obligations.*

behavior by the journalistic enterprises and the individuals who work for them in all their forms. So it has been since Robert Maynard Hutchins called his first meeting to order, and so it shall be in the coming years as the press and the law continue to deal with the evolving nature of information and how it is delivered.

10

Codes and Compromises

THE ADVOCATES OF newspapers, as essential bulwarks of a democratic society, have long believed that they provide an identity for the communities in which they are published. In the event that a paper closes down, local pride and cohesion diminish. A crucial voice may be silenced. One of the subtle attributes of local news is the possibility of greater self-knowledge based on the accounts of familiar experiences. Those who fear the attrition taking place in the current digital age are concerned about informed public opinion. For them, the question becomes—How do we strengthen print journalism?

Confidence in the American press has eroded steadily for many reasons—partisanship, sensationalism, and profit-seeking among them. Over the years in which mass communication grew in the late 19th and early 20th centuries, the idea of ethical codes frequently entered the discussion. Many newspapers, large and small, created written codes which were meant to encourage the support of readers and advertisers by professing high moral standards. Some of these codes were lyrically written and persuasive, but their usefulness seemed limited. Lawyers for the publishers cautioned against making promises that were difficult to keep. Readers and advertisers could accuse the owners and editors of not living up to their own rules. Reporters found that the high-minded ideas describing editorial product were not easily applied to every day reportorial problems. Adjusting to the pace and complexity of news, let alone political nuances and diverse opinions, so as to satisfy a written public declaration of presumed virtues, became more contentious and troubling than had been expected.

The press was accused of irresponsible excess, bias, fabrication and unfairness "cloaked" in the protective aura of the First Amendment. In that atmosphere, an ethics code could become a legal trap. Lawsuits were expensive, sometimes fatal. A small newspaper could be put out of business by legal costs. Even the most influential urban papers could be seriously damaged financially.

> *The press was accused of irresponsible excess, bias, fabrication and unfairness "cloaked" in the protective aura of the First Amendment. In that atmosphere, an ethics code could become a legal trap.*

New York Times v. Sullivan, the 1964 Supreme Court case which reshaped constitutional issues concerning the press, was preceded by an intense internal debate at the *New York*

Times before the publisher decided to risk litigation.

Newspapers in general had been subjected to harsh criticism from politicians and business leaders, but the elite handful of powerful national papers such as the *New York Times*, *The Washington Post*, and the *Wall Street Journal* were challenged by scholars and historians, who also went after the major television networks. All these prominent organizations were charged with failing to honor their professed principles for delivering news to the public with disinterested independence, clarity, and reliability.

There has always been a concern among thoughtful readers of the press that a moral compass and ethical codes are vital to the integrity of journalism. A moral compass is a guide to judgment, and codes are, in effect, a contract between the parties. State-wide codes appeared in the 1920s, including Missouri, South Dakota, Oregon and Washington. Individual newspapers such as the *Brooklyn Eagle*, *Christian Science Monitor*, *Detroit News* and *Seattle Times* produced their own codes. These were varied in style and content—some, according to University of Illinois media scholar Clifford Christians, were explicit ("always verify names"), others inspirational ("be vigorous but not vicious").

At its first meeting, the American Society of Newspaper Editors (ASNE) voted to compose an institutional code. In 1923 it unanimously approved "The Canons of Journalism." It was adopted by many other journalism organizations and stimulated discussion in trade journals such as the *Journalism*

Quarterly, which published a series of pieces on education and codes as the only way to make journalism an "honorable profession." Some writers compared journalism to medicine and law. The notion that journalism could earn a "professional standing" never really took hold (as examined in earlier essays) because it did not provide an agreed set of texts and a required educational training, along with a body of work and appropriate examinations. The journalist is often self-appointed. Anyone can tuck a press card into his hat band and call himself a journalist. The online operations have augmented the opportunities and diversified the credentials. There are more reporters working on "analysis," and increasing numbers of "platforms"—print, video and the Internet. That diversified environment does not lend itself to ethical codes.

At its first meeting, the American Society of Newspaper Editors (ASNE) voted to compose an institutional code. In 1923 it unanimously approved "The Canons of Journalism."

There is also less audible concern in these times for establishing journalism professionally at the same level as medicine and law, as was the case in the 1920s. One major issue has been part of the conversation since codes were first proposed—accountability.

It has been widely accepted in the discussion of journalism, ethics and the concept of self-regulation, that to be accountable we must acknowledge that we can be called to judgment and charged with not fulfilling our obligations.

Accountability also involves possible punishment. When actual laws are broken the courts will determine the consequences. On a moral level accountability involves public censure and the disapproval of the community to which we are accountable. The distinctions between *legal* and *moral* can in themselves become an issue.

The various codes established at newspapers, magazines, broadcast companies and journalistic organizations called on members to censure violations, even try to prevent them, but rarely provided defined penalties. Over the years, speeches and letters commonly warned against "enforcement." Such measures, it was often said, would produce "paranoia" and "abuses." The broadcast industry codes, critics pointed out, seemed to focus on government interference, but all the codes favored "self-regulation."

If we believe that the only authentic agent of a moral decision is an individual, then individuals who voluntarily join institutions, or organizations, can and must bear some responsibility for the actions and policies of the collective they belong to. But it makes little sense to blame a whole institution for the mistakes, or wrongdoing, of a few people responsible for a particular action.

Can ethical standards be defined by a group (professional or aspirational) with the larger society in mind? Furthermore, without a realistic sense of accountability, to be specific, can a news organization provide reliable public affairs reporting within the context of ethical standards? Finally, can they explain their perception to the appropriate audience consistently and coherently? We are left wondering what the effect of ethics has on the press when it covers such sensitive issues as poverty, racism, environment and crime.

But it makes little sense to blame a whole institution for the mistakes, or wrongdoing, of a few people responsible for a particular action.

There are distinguished commentators who believe a system of "normative" ethics could reflect goals and aspirations rather than self-regulation as a response to potential government interference. The ambition is to bring the consumer/citizen into the process of determining what is the best moral outcome. A collaboration of citizens and a free press would be a proactive and accountable process—in theory. It would at least precede violations rather than confront them after the fact.

There is no way of assuring ethical behavior. In contemplating the behavior of the press—burdened as it is by partisanship, commercialism, and the fragmentation of the digital universe—the composition of unenforceable codes, or the creation of shared normative ethics programs, will not bring convincing standards to the modern marketplace of information.

Education is the only effective remedy in sight. Education can make the consumer, the provider, and the regulator more knowledgeable, more discerning, and more ethical. It cannot make them always right or wise, but it can move them in that direction.

The schools and departments of journalism at our colleges are contributing to the consciousness of the practitioners and giving them some sense of ethical judgment—along with the roots and history of the principles and values which make ethics both essential and enduring.

Casper Yost, editor of the *Saint Louis Globe Democrat* in the 1920s, helped the American Society of Newspaper Editors (ASNE) to develop their "Canons of Ethics." Among his admonitions was this comment:

> "Individual standards will always remain individual and continue to be as varied as individual nature until the profession of journalism, through collective consideration and action, establishes a code of ethics by which all journalistic conduct can be measured."

He was right in part one, wrong in part two. The individual journalistic standards will always be individual, yes. But no code has been written that can bring talented, educated individuals into lockstep. Education can help them find common ground, and education can give them the confidence to choose the high standards necessary for the pursuit of truth. More than 2,600 years ago Plato declared that education is the "one great thing". It is a statement that may have suffered a bit in translation but has not lost its meaning or its relevance.

11

Is Anybody Home?

ACCORDING TO PLATO, his teacher—a chunky, heroic war veteran named Socrates—was opposed to handwriting. Socrates, who earned his living as a carver of tombstones, had developed an enduring curiosity about knowledge—the demonstrable and logical understanding of the world around him. He met frequently with groups of young Athenian men to discuss philosophy and politics, employing a method called dialectics. Dialectics began with cross examination. He would offer a question to his young followers, listen to their answers, and then ask more questions that might deflate some arguments and build on others. He was seeking truth and logic in the process.

"Knowledge" said he, "is virtue."

"The knowers," Plato extrapolated, "should be the rulers." They should need no laws or legislatures, because their virtuousness assured wise and just policies. In that context, Socrates resisted writing. He never wrote anything himself.

What little we know of him we learned primarily from Plato's recollections. In one of Plato's dialogues, presumably between Socrates and his students, called *Phaedrus*, Socrates observes that writing will weaken memory and produce only a "semblance" of wisdom, "but no real judgment." Socrates, it seems, feared that written words would be a substitute for what we used to carry around in our heads. The oral tradition was then at its peak—around 450 B.C.

Memory is the issue, and in examining the function of brain and mind now in the digital age, memory is still an issue. Do we need our memory if we have the massive databanks available in our computers? "Just Google it," we say.

Aristotle, Plato's most eminent student, placed great value on education, but he believed no one could know it all. There were in his view no "Philosopher Kings." Law was the one "Just King," and laws would be written by educated men in the best interest of all the citizens of any state. A good education, in Aristotle's view, would provide each citizen at least an "acquaintance-ship" with every branch of knowledge. In a viable democracy, if government requires the consent of the governed—and Aristotle believed it must—education was quintessential. It nourishes the mind.

> *Memory is the issue, and in examining the function of brain and mind now in the digital age, memory is still an issue. Do we need our memory if we have the massive databanks available in our computers? "Just Google it," we say.*

Mind over matter has been a central interest of intellectuals since the birth of scientific inquiry. Writing beyond record keeping developed slowly. It was accelerated by the printing press, a device that could be replicated and widely used. Gutenberg, its inventor, had also designed the molds for movable metal type, and inks of many colors, which he used beautifully in his earliest printed books—elaborate editions of the Bible. But it took more than 150 years after that for the first publication of what came to be called novels. *Don Quixote*, by Cervantes, was the earliest known story among them, published in 1605. Newspapers appeared for the first time around 1609.

Reaction to the printing press was not entirely favorable. Similar to the apprehension of Socrates and his students regarding handwriting, many scholars believed printing would make errors permanent. Fear of blasphemy, or inaccuracy or falsehood also animated opposition to the printing press. Changing traditional practices (as already noted) suffered resistance, but those that persisted could be seminal. Philosopher Francis Bacon, in 1620, wrote that printing, magnets, and gun power were the three inventions that "changed the whole face and state of things throughout the world."

In the 18th century the poet Alexander Pope, among many other writers, called the printing press "a scourge for the sins of the learned." In the 19th century, Tolstoy stated in his monumental work *War and Peace* that the "dissemination of printed matter" was "the most powerful of ignorance's weapons."

For most of human history, changes in technology and behavior moved incrementally, but two communications devices in modern times have made remarkably swift inroads—television and the Internet. Television entered half of all American homes in its first eight years—during the 1950s and early 60s. The computer has not made that great a penetration since the debut of the IBM-PC, but its influence has grown very rapidly.

Meanwhile, it is estimated that half the planet's population—three billion people, give or take—spend more time watching television than any other leisure pursuit, and much of that medium can, and will, be "streaming" film and video onto websites one way or another, as has already begun. The Internet, however, is the most significant of all the new technologies because it can change how we think. A five-year research project, completed in England during the 1990's, combining the facilities of the British Library and a consortium of English universities, revealed that:

> "It is clear that users are not reading in the traditional sense. Indeed, there are signs that new forms of 'readings' are emerging as users 'power browse' horizontally through titles, contents pages, and abstracts, going for quick wins. It also seems they go online to avoid reading in the traditional sense."

A professor who participated in the research projects, reported "I can't read *War and Peace* anymore. Even a blog of more than three or four paragraphs is too long."

The most common finding in a dozen of these reports

made by scholars and technicians is the "deep reading" loss. The digital technology invites jumping to the next site, or the next link. Studies of the human brain reveal new configurations, nerve cells making new connections in the brains of those who are regularly immersed in online work.

The Internet, however, is the most significant of all the new technologies because it can change how we think.

The scientists who have conducted this work here and abroad believe that the diminution of "deep reading" erodes "deep thinking" and therefore the ability to deal with critical reasoning—which requires reflection, meditation, and creativity—all functions of the human mind. At the very least, individual consumers of the Internet must consider the necessity for due diligence in their choice of data. When Google offers dozens of citations in regard to a single query, the weight of examining the full range of answers and making choices falls on the individual consumer.

A "World Wide Web," which is now virtually in place, is seen by some as a provider of unlimited information services. It is seen by others as an inexorable engine of fragmentation. What it does to the function of independent deep thinking has not yet been fully determined, but the evidence clearly points to the increasing inability to read in depth. Engagement with the Internet, according to extensive reporting, seems always to promote a state of partial attention.

I can attest to similar findings anecdotally. Students I have taught during the past 20 years are reading books and newspapers less, using the digital instruments more. The quality of writing, as seen in their essays, did not deteriorate greatly but how much content is "lifted" from the Internet is difficult to measure. The convenient accessibility of information and analysis provided online makes *plagiarism*, as earlier generations understood it, a minor offense. Young people who have used computers since kindergarten regard the product on the screen as public domain. *Attribution* needs to be given much more attention. Creative thinking may be, on the other hand, changing in both form and process. Computational acceleration is the hallmark. The question not yet answered is "At what speed does wisdom come to us?"

As an experiment, I divided my classes in half and each week one group would prepare by using a blog they created for the purpose of discussing the assigned reading. The other half of the class would conduct a discussion, Socratically, in the classroom. The following week, the two groups would reverse the procedure.

Young people who have used computers since kindergarten regard the product on the screen as public domain.

My participation would be, I thought, as a moderator. I expected the classroom debate to be the preferred method. As it turned out, that was not the case. All but one student reported that they were far more comfortable working on the computer. They were very clear about two points: (1) on the computer, they were not being observed, and they could revisit the text whenever they wanted to change their "postings" in response to digital comments from other members of the team. (2) They had very little experience over the years in classroom debate, or declamation, and felt intimidated by "eloquent students" and/or "the professor." They also confirmed that a computer has been central to their education since childhood.

> *Working in isolation with the ability to check facts and rewrite commentary is obviously less challenging than delivering opinions and evaluations in the clamor of classroom debate.*

The "postings" to the student blog were forwarded to me each week and I read them all. These "postings" were almost always more articulate and polished than the ad hoc comments made in class. This was understandable in one sense, but disturbing in another.

Working in isolation with the ability to check facts and rewrite commentary is obviously less challenging than delivering opinions and evaluations in the clamor of classroom debate. But to be intimidated by the prospect of tapping into memory and judgment based on the reading of a text, or responding to the reviews of classmates spontaneously, seems astonishing to those of us who grew up without Google. Surprise, however, is not the most important reaction. Concern for cognition—for the learning process—is more worrying. That concern may be modified over time by the evidence of learning in a new and different manner, which is the point of these ruminations.

Richard Foreman, a playwright who participated in the British research on the effects of digital education, wrote: "As we are emptied of our inner repertory of dense cultural inheritance, we seem to be turning into 'pancake people,' spread wide and thin as we connect with the vast network of information accessed by the mere touch of a button."

The world of print—of books and magazines and newspapers—which was our primary source of information for five centuries after the invention of the printing press, was based in the words of Professor Neil Postman on "logic, sequence, history, expression, objectivity, detachment, and discipline." The Internet, now overtaking print, in the words of writer Nicholas Carr, puts its emphasis on "immediacy, simultaneity, contingency, subjectivity, disposability, and, above all, speed."

Therein, I think, is a major challenge we face in the future of education, journalism, and a healthy democracy. Computer scientists, in their explorations, viewed the possibilities of the Web as a tool that would enhance the power of the brain. In theory, the human mind would shape the enlarged intelligence by deep thinking and critical reasoning. If however, the *mind* is not dominant, we return to the question, *Do we become tools of our tools?*

At stake is the quality of education, journalism and what is called "the national conversation." Either we master the World Wide Web without losing our ability and appetite to interpret texts and make connections propelled by memory and thought—the core of a liberal arts education—or we slip into a dependency on the "instantly available" data of the Net.

What may become unavailable is the educated, articulate personality who can write with irony and nuance, cite evocative literary allusions, and produce the concentration that creates imaginative new ideas. We are what we are because we make choices that determine our destiny. Nobel Laureate Roger Sperry once wrote, "Mind controls matter. It is superior to brain in the capacity to will, intend, command, and direct."

The mind lives on memory. If we let memory and critical reasoning whither because we can click on Google, once or many times, and it will remember for us, what will we become? Carr offers one answer—all technological change is generational. "The full effect of a new technology is felt most vividly when those who grow up with it become adults."

There are many technological and philosophical issues that the news media will face in the next few years. Two of them are fundamentally important but nonetheless will be shaped by public opinion and economic unpredictability.

> *The mind lives on memory. If we let memory and critical reasoning whither because we can click on Google, once or many times, and it will remember for us, what will we become?*

They are the so-called "net neutrality" of the free and open Internet, and the control of editorial content at the major digital platforms.

The FCC at the end of 2017 voted along party lines to relax—

if not eliminate—government restraints on the large telecom companies such as Verizon and AT&T. Law suits followed almost immediately from small online business groups, and individuals, essentially charging that they will be priced out of the market. Litigation may take years and will probably alter the FCC proposal to some extent, but the issues are of vital significance to start-up ventures. Claims have been made that Google and Facebook—among others—would not have emerged so strongly without "net neutrality" which gave the new ideas the same access to online marketing as given to the large digital corporations.

At the heart of the debate is the original intent of the Internet to be, in effect, a *public utility* as opposed to being a tool of private enterprise. The FCC majority took the position that free markets would keep the competition balanced.

As to the content of programming, and political coverage, concern has been rising about hate groups such as the white nationalists and the neo-Nazis, along with other extremist organizations which use the Internet to recruit new members and influence elections. The 2016 campaigns were seriously influenced online by massive—often automated—commercials, misinformation, and deliberate falsehoods distorting political activity in America and in Europe. Some of the platforms claimed they were unaware of the magnitude

> *At the heart of the debate is the original intent of the Internet to be, in effect, a* public *utility as opposed to being a tool of private enterprise.*

of propaganda and distortion until the election was over. Subsequently they banned such groups as the neo-Nazis and the Ku Klux Klan. They also announced that hate organizations and deliberate fake news operators would not be allowed access to advertising revenue. There was, however, no comprehensive and clear policy to prevent extremist, anti-American entities from getting online. Google and

The 2016 campaigns were seriously influenced online by massive—often automated— commercials, misinformation, and deliberate falsehoods distorting political activity in America and in Europe.

Facebook ultimately hired large numbers of people to monitor material coming to their platforms, and reject "inappropriate" messages.

Meanwhile, in Europe, several countries led by Germany and England drafted regulations that imposed sizable fines meant to discourage the "trolls" who posted objectionable or false material. How this kind of menace can be dealt with, and who will try to control it, are questions that will not be easily answered. The infamous public parade of white nationalists and Nazis at Charlottesville, Virginia, in the summer of 2017, not far from the University of Virginia, shocked many Americans. Edmund Burke's prophetic warning that evil will triumph if good people merely look the other way seems to have been forgotten.

Hatemongers were emboldened at Charlottesville, and elsewhere, during 2016 and onward. The presumed constituency called "decent Americans" may turn away, or they may show their resolve in future elections. The responsible press will have to make hard decisions on their editorial pages, but the issues will not go away. What many Americans have taken for granted is the strength of their Constitution and the rule of law. It is a strength that needs the nourishment of reliable information, and the motivation to find it—a task that seems particularly suitable for journalism.

Neither goal can be assured. I have already cited due diligence and education as the most reliable sources of truth in the age of distortion and falsehood. Untruth

> *What many Americans have taken for granted is the strength of their Constitution and the rule of law.*

festers poisonously in the environment of social media, ideological websites, and enormous audiences available through online platforms.

The use of technological methods to reach mass circulation with carefully devised propaganda, political innuendo, and bigotry has devalued fact-based evidence. How such messages are inflicted on public opinion might be exposed and rejected primarily through education in all its forms. Many school systems are already introducing courses which examine the issues surrounding how digital technology is used for malevolent purposes. The media companies are learning more every day about so called fake news—how to detect deception, how to avoid it, and where to look for offenders—including foreign interests. Education takes place on the job for journalists, assisted by fact checking services. To identify and protect the truth, we now need to employ organized due diligence and education as basic methods for supporting accuracy and intelligent interpretation of news and public information.

It is, of course, common sense to take advantage of every means of filtering out manipulation and falsity online. But the difference in context and technique that currently applies to the flow of information on public affairs, the size of audiences reached, and the speed of transmission has altered reality far more seriously and irreversibly than in any previous period of American history. Put simply—faceless, nameless agents have been able to reach—and misinform—millions of American voters overnight with material that can do great harm in a manner that cannot be corrected or recalled within a timeframe that countervails the damage done.

Education as a means of "putting things right" is a complicated task that is not something new. A well informed electorate has always been an aspiration of the experiment we call democracy. How we assure reliable information in the era of artificial intelligence, and virulent tribalism, is a challenge we now face—with too little confidence that there is a ready solution.

12

Fomenting Fake News

THE PRACTICE OF misinformation and deception is not a recent phenomenon. What has been called "fake news" has been around for a long time. Storytelling, mythology, propaganda, and other labels such as "adroit misdirection" go back to the ancient civilizations.

Two interesting precursors to fake news, as it is practiced currently, are worth noting. One of these (largely self-induced) was given a profound and timeless analysis by Walter Lippmann in the 1920s. He called it "the pictures in our heads." Lippmann envisioned a kind of "pseudo-reality" created in the mind when we are aware of distant events that are "out of reach" and "out of sight." To make some connection we produce "pictures inside our head." The problem created by pseudo-reality is that we also make decisions based on those pictures, which can be misleading. The consequences of pseudo-reality take place in an *actual* reality with unexpected contrasts in fact and judgment.

Lippmann understood the reasons why these pictures so often mislead us in dealing with the actual newsworthy activity outside our experience.

"Those pictures," he wrote, "which are acted upon by groups of people, or by individuals acting in the name of groups, are Public Opinion with capital letters."

Lippmann envisioned a kind of "pseudo-reality" created in the mind when we are aware of distant events that are "out of reach" and "out of sight."

Lippmann deplored the frequent failure of the pictures we create to produce an accurate and reliable impression of reality. Among the reasons for confusion, he pointed out, were (and still are) a factor he called "artificial censorships." These include the limitations of social contact; little time each day for reflecting on public affairs; the need to compress information into short messages; making a small vocabulary express a complicated issue; and the fear of facing those facts which would seem to threaten the established routine of our lives.

All these factors influence how we form our opinions, what we think of as truth, and eventually how we vote. There is a remarkable similarity between Lippmann's view of public opinion in the 1920s, and the formation of public opinion in the first part of the 21st century.

An interesting example took place in the 1980s when the Reagan administration found itself in a strained relationship with Libya and its flamboyant dictator Moammar Gadhafi.

Secretary of State George Shultz saw it as "pretty close to war." In that conflict, Shultz condoned the use of deception, or what he called "psychological warfare."

Gadhafi was believed to have hijacked a Pan American world Airways plane in Pakistan. "I know of no decision to have people go out and tell lies," Shultz said."I think, however, if there are ways to make Gadhafi nervous, why shouldn't we?"

He further observed that the American press liked to focus on United States Navy actions which, in this case, could make Gadhafi fear his country might be invaded. "You people," Shultz said, "in the news business enjoy not allowing the US to do anything in secret if you can help it. So we can absolutely bank on the fact that if the fleet does something or other, you will scream. Gadhafi will hear it, and the fleet may, or may not be getting ready to do something."

Mr. Shultz was asked if there was a strategic decision to "disinform." The reporter called it a "very serious charge."

"Why is this a charge?" Shultz asked. "If I was a private citizen reading about it, and I read that my government was trying to confuse somebody who was conducting terrorist acts and murdering Americans, I would say, 'Gee, I hope it is true.' I don't see why you think this is a charge."

As a result of the attention given to such questions, the spokesman for the State Department, Bernard Kalb, a veteran newsman, resigned to protest what he considered to be a US *disinformation* program designed to undermine Gadhafi.

"I don't want my own credibility to be caught up, or

subsumed, in the controversy," Kalb stated. "The controversy may vanish but, when you are sitting alone, it does not go away."

He nonetheless refused to confirm the actual existence of a disinformation effort. Several journalists serving as spokesmen for government departments had resigned from earlier administrations for similar reasons, prompting Hodding Carter III, who had been a well-known spokesmen from 1972-1980, to say he found it "refreshing that in a town full of careerists someone decided that what brought him into government is what took him out—integrity."

There were those who would argue such decisions are not simple to make, nor characterized by certitude. Many today in the struggle against terrorism would defend deception. If the enemy uses deception and misinformation—particularly online—similar tactics by us may be justified. The moral issue centers on the determination of when we are at war. Fake news in domestic politics is another matter.

Regarding wartime deception, when ISIS forces were heading for the Iraqi city of Mosul, they used Internet technology to release more than 40,000 tweets a day, deluging the region with false stories of conquest and punishment. This suggested power and momentum of a wildly inaccurate dimension, but nonetheless frightening and confusing for local residents. The magnitude made it appear that Iraq was collapsing.

Current manipulation of so-called social media is being adapted by urban gangs and other small groups, as well as large political factions and military forces. As already noted, broad-based reporting has confirmed that the Internet can educate and bring people together, but it can also misinform, enlarge hatreds and ideologies already festering, and incite violence.

American "white nationalist" groups, according to research on extremism conducted at George Washington University, have increased 600% since 2012. The Russian government has been deeply involved for decades in the misinformation business and has created a news service called *Russia Today* that is often the most popular outlet of its kind on *YouTube*. It broadcasts in English, Arabic, and Spanish, along with its regular Russian, French and German reporting. Behind all this propaganda and fake news is a vast army of writers and editors who put an outpouring of material together with the help of government funding and a mission to mislead and distort. *Atlantic Magazine* reported how Russian "troll factories," as cyber warfare efforts are called, planted rumors and assertions on social media indicating that American nuclear weapons kept in Turkey would be moved to a base in Romania, where (in fact) a US anti-missile system was located. The apparent goal of this fabricated story was to encourage the unraveling of US/Turkey relations and arouse the resentment of Romanians who feared American military activity in their country.

> *American "white nationalist" groups, according to research on extremism conducted at George Washington University, have increased 600% since 2012.*

This kind of plotting and maneuvering, utilizing fake news, is intrinsic to cyber warfare, and the confusion it causes among analysts and reporters has been harnessed by the Russians in particular, but others as well. The consequences, in addition to the threat to American security interests, are the responsibility it places on the intelligence services, and on the news media that seek an accurate account of world affairs. Once more the concept of due diligence appears, and with it the intensifying need for competent, well-trained news reporters.

The narrators of information, particularly in regard to public issues, have always carried some baggage—presuppositions, prejudices, or political bias among them. But the environment in which information achieves power has become vastly extended and enlarged; along with the technology that provides access to so many people swiftly and incessantly. In that evolving technological environment fake news can be a powerful infection—and sometimes profitable for those who produce it.

Platforms such as Twitter and Facebook, along with websites and blogs, are exploited by individuals and special interest groups to engage "followers" who may be like-minded on political and social issues. Without any real evidence—let alone proof—a fake news story can become "viral" by using provocative messages that cater to the beliefs of identifiable, targeted audiences. ISIS has successfully recruited potential *jihadists* to radical Islam by fabricating Internet news stories.

Domestically, white supremacists, nationalists, neo-Nazis, the Klu Klux Klan, and fragmentary hate groups have found supporters on the Internet. Researchers, and academic studies, have for many years demonstrated that Internet formats gather people with shared attitudes and inclinations who inevitably move towards more extreme versions of their beliefs if they are exposed primarily (or only) to similar views. Because of

Without any real evidence—let alone proof—a fake news story can become "viral" by using provocative messages that cater to the beliefs of identifiable, targeted audiences.

ongoing research here and abroad, we know that without diversity, or debate, like-minded people move to the extremes. We also know that people exposed to diverse views usually move to the center. Fake news stories are more acceptable to the extremists.

Socrates examined fakery in his peripatetic conversations with the young Athenian men who were dazzled by his skepticism. His "argumentative reasoning" would be useful today, but not unless it is applied before Twitter or Facebook, or both, have carried a fake news distortion beyond recall or correction. Deliberately composed misinformation has become a useful weapon for special interests, political operatives, and marketing strategists. The process can range from blatant public statements to a "tweet," such as those frequently issued during the 2016 political campaigns.

The common currency of fake news is a "meme"—a term

that was identified by Richard Dawkins as a "unit of cultural transmission." In a *New Yorker* profile, Dawkins says that "computers are increasingly tied together in electronic mail exchange…. Now, however ridiculous what you are saying is, if you make it *memetically* successful, something really bad can spread through the culture."(*Emphasis added*)

The most dangerous reaction to fake news content is the rising number of attacks on the mainstream media. The idea that the traditional press is untrustworthy and the captive of elite—almost always described as liberal—establishments, has resonated on the Internet. Hate groups and some conservative segments (not by any means sharing the same views) have nevertheless found common ground in their hostility towards the mainstream media. That predisposition seems to mischaracterize the press as monolithic in its editorial views. Such hyperbole is one of the core factors in the partisan divisiveness afflicting American political life.

The fake news device can be so outrageously unfounded, it is puzzling that an educated person would be willing to believe it. During the 2016 presidential campaign, fake news stories were sufficiently preposterous to cause skepticism at the very least. They were, however, constructed and distributed on Internet platforms in the compressed, assertive style that would appeal to preconceptions and bigotry—and did. How many votes were influenced by such material is now—and will be for some time to come—the subject of considerable research. The fact that Mrs. Clinton received just about 3 million more votes than Mr. Trump has been somewhat lost in the mists of carefully nourished mistrust of any factual data produced by the "elite," establishment press.

The Oxford University Project on Algorithms, Computational Propaganda and Digital Politics (a painfully timely title) completed a report that was published in November, 2016. It examined all the components in its long name. Among many revealing statistics the report emphasized the use of "chatbots"—software programs designed to send messages on social media such as Twitter. The message content would be a topic identified with a word or name preceded by a "hashtag" symbol. Philip Howard, a co-author of the report, describes the chatbot messages as mechanisms to spread confusion or fake news, but not useful for serious commentary or debate.

Meanwhile, Google, Twitter and Facebook are planning to ban websites that distribute fake news from using online advertising services. Presumably, advertising will not be placed in sites that have provided misleading or false content. This may diminish profit and the number of fake messages, but not prevent them altogether. The individual consumer may still need to pursue independent due diligence to find reliable news in the digital jungle.

The Oxford researchers confirmed a number of elements of messaging formats believed to have developed over time, but not yet fully explored. In this study the researchers examined a pool of more than nineteen million postings on Twitter. They identified automated postings among the "accounts" that were active fifty or more times each day. Highly automated accounts, according to the report, averaged more than one thousand tweets a day. These accounts generated over 430,000 tweets in the first nine days of November, 2016—the period covered by this study. An earlier report had found that political chatbots played a significant role in England when the voting on Brexit was publically debated. The researchers created the term "computational propaganda" to define the role of deceptive social media messaging.

They also estimated that in the American election the Twitter-style of campaigning involved automated delivery that flowed into online traffic with automated messages. That in itself produced fake news distortions. Obviously absent from such "strategies" is the careful deliberation that accompanies any concern for accuracy or truth.

The question arises with great frequency—what is the responsibility of the large corporations that are the principal owners of social media? As one example, Facebook has more than two billion users worldwide. It can exert incalculable influence in shaping public opinion, and therefore elections. When that influence moves into international affairs, governments might intervene and usually do. Could the United States government, in the name of security, nationalize or censor social media? In the current political environment that seems a realistic possibility. The war on terror has no borders.

Whether the issue is content or reach, any effort to restrain social media will have constitutional implications. The conflict philosophically, in the context of free speech, is familiar territory, but technological changes have created dilemmas of size and control and impact never imagined before. *How* digital information is delivered, and *what* it says can alter the course of war, negotiations, and political outcomes so significantly that history seems to be separating itself from the past and beginning a new reality.

Could the United States government, in the name of security, nationalize or censor social media?

The consumer is obliged to evaluate and determine the truthfulness of the news media he selects. He may one day be helped by an accreditation organization made up of retired journalists and academics who could certify the integrity and ethical standards of responsible purveyors of news—print, broadcast or Internet. The formation of such a body will, of course, require widespread agreement among news companies. The consumer could look for credentials awarded by the monitors, not unlike those given to universities, hospitals, and other institutions in our society that serve the public interest. Obviously the prestige and competence of the accreditation committee would have to be unquestionable. However it evolves, some means of assuring public confidence is necessary to challenge the radical concepts of the self-appointed, "politically incorrect" creators of the "new Fourth Estate." The traditional enterprises have their work cut out for them.

After all, it is the individual who has embraced the fragmentation and, for many, the *isolation* of digital instruments.

But the new devices bring no authority to abandon the search for truth, or the rules of evidence, or the moral compass that once resonated in the vanishing newsrooms of responsible newspapers and broadcast stations. To replace the "filtering" provided by news rooms, due diligence on the part of consumers is needed, but surely a hard sell. More likely to succeed are the fact-checking services, and media literacy programs in public schools and colleges.

The consumer could look for credentials awarded by the monitors, not unlike those given to universities, hospitals, and other institutions in our society that serve the public interest.

The multi-media news cycle has feverishly adopted technology, but it has forgotten about *time to think*. That deficiency becomes an open door for fake news. Winston Churchill once said, "In wartime, truth is so precious that she should always be attended by a bodyguard of lies."

In the current information wars, many have wondered whether our technology would truly surpass our humanity. Now we may find out.

13

The Spirit of Liberty

AN ENORMOUSLY RESPECTED federal judge named Learned Hand—often called the greatest judge who didn't make it to the Supreme Court—spoke to a large crowd in New York City on "I Am an American Day," in 1944. World War II was still being fiercely fought as he spoke, and judge Hand described the need to defeat Nazi Germany. His audience included many people who were seeking citizenship in the United States.

What was the reason for coming to America, he asked. Liberty, he answered. "Freedom from oppression, freedom from want, freedom to be ourselves." He went on to question whether we rely too much on constitutions, laws and courts. "Liberty lies in the hearts of men and women...the spirit of liberty is the spirit which is not too sure that it is right; the spirit of liberty is the spirit that seeks to understand the minds of other men and women; the spirit of liberty is the spirit which weighs their interest alongside its own without bias. The spirit of liberty remembers that not even a sparrow falls to earth unheeded...."

Learned Hand was a man of the law who knew that without the motivation to understand and serve the purpose of laws "with conscience and courage" we become a society where "freedom is the possession of only a savage few."

There was in Learned Hand a vision of decency and kindness as part of a social compact. It can be assumed that he had read the works of John Stuart Mill. It might also be assumed that he and Mill would agree on a great many ideas regarding human rights. On the notion of certitude they surely would have lifted a glass to salute a common bond of skepticism and openness.

British philosopher Isaiah Berlin, who had a lifelong interest in freedom and was an advocate of Mill's views, observed that no other writers had an impact "more immediate and no less permanent" than Mill's declarations concerning freedom.

For Mill the truth was always a work in progress—never finished. It could be altered or amended or corrected by time and unexpected discovery. It was therefore not advisable to treat it as a certainty. Reading Learned Hand's 1944 speech and thinking about John Stuart Mill's elegant treatise on liberty makes an interesting continuum. Truth may change, as it so often has, but the wisdom of both these men has endured.

Journalism at its best constantly seeks the truth but may never know when the search has ended. Mill wanted truth-seeking to leave the gate open so that some new idea might be added, or some error might be removed. He did not want conventional wisdom untested by opposing or diverse views.

The structure of truth, and its importance to the public interest, has been central to any discussion of democracy, but not always the primary concern of the news media. Scholars and commentators such as Hutchins have challenged the press to recognize a social responsibility, which was not always defined in the 20th century as news became corporatized and profits grew. The irony of a constitutional protection for a profit making private enterprise provoked serious attempts to regulate the press. The advent of radio and television stimulated calls for licensing and legislative measures. Many efforts were made to establish a "New First Amendment" that would deal with innovative electronic means of communication. The electronic press has always been vulnerable to charges that it is a public utility in private hands.

Taken together print and electronic news—including now the Internet and the giant corporations that control digital distribution systems (e.g., Google and Facebook)—are involved in industrial operations that reach around the world. They cannot escape, however, the moral responsibility of controlling the dissemination of knowledge and news vital to the political and economic concerns of ordinary people, wherever they may be.

The electronic press has always been vulnerable to charges that it is a public utility in private hands.

For the nations that call themselves democracies, there

is a ceaseless struggle to satisfy the information needs of diverse populations. Alexander Meiklejon, educator and social philosopher, wrote in 1960 that "human interests are in conflict with one another. They cannot all be realized. We cannot make the common good by simply adding them all together. To give play to one of them means often to deny play to others. And for this reason, the public interest cannot be merely the totality of the private interests. It is, of necessity, an organization of them, a selection and arrangement based upon judgment of relative values and mutual implications."

The avoidance of certainty is a condition enlightened journalists usually find acceptable because experience has taught them to expect change. Facts may withstand questioning and not suffer refutation. Conclusions and assumptions are more vulnerable.

The frequently cited *New York Times v Sullivan* case in 1964 had also settled another issue that had lingered obscurely since the ratification of the federal documents, and the amendments in 1791. How does the United States Constitution interact with the separate state constitutions? The Alabama Supreme Court in 1963 had declared that "libel is beneath constitutional protection." The US Supreme Court rejected that assertion and made it clear that the expression of opinion or debate on "public questions" must be protected by the First Amendment.

In effect this meant debate in public affairs could allow statements that were not always true. A plaintiff would have to prove both *falsity* and *malice*. The Court stipulated that a judge would be required to review all the evidence in advance to determine the validity of any complaint before scheduling a trial. Though malice would not be easily proven, blatant falseness calculatedly expressed in contradiction of known facts could not avoid prosecution. The laws in many state constitutions—particularly in the south—had provided broadly defined sedition violations, often with very serious penalties. These state constitutional laws had been for many years enforced without reference to First Amendment or Fourteenth Amendment provisions. The *New York Times v. Sullivan* opinion reset the clock. The federal constitution at long last had become the primary voice on all matters affecting fundamental rights belonging to the citizens of the United States.

One of the significant consequences of that case was the validation of the "right to be wrong" tradition, as many lawyers called

> *Though malice would not be easily proven, blatant falseness calculatedly expressed in contradiction of known facts could not avoid prosecution.*

it. The Court's admonition that political debates should be robust, and errors of fact might occur, protected space for a heated argument. Deliberate falsehoods and "actual malice," however, remained out of bounds. Determining where the line is drawn continues to be a judicial issue.

The devaluation of truth in recent years has allowed freedom of speech and press to be used as a license for deception.

Partisan debate has often become malicious slander, or crude innuendo. The organized "trolls" have harnessed Internet platforms to distribute targeted propaganda and falsification—much of it from foreign interests such as Russia, China, North Korea and Iran. Their messages in the past decade were—and are—designed to affect voting, and augment divisiveness in American society. The right to be wrong has been overtaken by digital malevolence.

The Bill of Rights (the first ten amendments) had been considered a restraint only on Federal powers (i.e., "Congress shall make no law..."). The Fourteenth Amendment (1868) was, in the view of most constitutional scholars, meant to apply the Bill of Rights to the states.

The Constitutional Convention discussions frequently cited the history of the ancient republics. Civility and compromise may not have been entirely the gift of Greek or Roman history, but the connections were evident. The authors of "The Age of Federalism," Stanley Elkins and Eric McKittrick, point out that the words and offices—"President," "Senate," "Congress"— echo the terms used by the ancients. James Madison looked to classical history (not the contemporary political parties) when he said in the House of Representatives "The more simple, the more Republican we are in our manners, the more rational dignity we shall require."

The spirit of liberty was not always so high-minded. Several of the newly born American states withheld their votes on the ratification of the Constitution, in their own interest, until a Bill of Rights was enumerated. These were largely personal rights, but they reflected the division of thought, then and now, regarding where ultimate power resides in a democratic Republic—federal government, state government, or sovereign people.

As to the resistance in the ratification process, Madison observed: "We ought not to disregard their inclination, but, on principles of amity and moderation, confirm to their wishes and expressly declare the great rights of mankind."

Madison realized early on that the individual state legislatures would ignore or circumvent the Federal Bill of Rights. And so they did. Sedition laws survived in the state constitutions, and in the 1830s southern states prosecuted newspaper publishers who had dared to criticize local government.

The "spirit of liberty" stirs in the vastly expanded digital media as it always has in any form of a free press, but it struggles against the currents of commercial opportunism and fabrication. The new technology provides no special protection for truth telling. Its vast reach ironically opens the door to fake news and falsehoods. Donald Trump called the press "the enemy of the people." He has also utilized social media to circumvent the mainline press.

The online press uses platforms to reach its audiences. Those platforms are privately owned corporations that can legally establish rules and standards regarding the information conveyed by their equipment. It would seem evident that the best remedy for fraud or deception in the messages communicated on widely used platforms is discipline imposed by the proprietors of the distribution systems. That discipline can be based on a moral compass or an instinct for self-preservation—probably both. Any company that permitted fake news or other objectionable products to be sent to hundreds of thousands—often millions—of subscribers could be inviting legal actions (including

The new technology provides no special protection for truth telling. Its vast reach ironically opens the door to fake news and falsehoods.

fines) and damaged reputations that would inevitably erode their bottom line.

Companies such as Google and Facebook take such matters seriously, but they have reacted slowly and quietly so far. The possibility of strong prohibitions as a company policy, expressed publically and clearly made part of contracts, may develop in the future. The potential damage that can be carried by wide-spread use of fake news will probably bring government regulation into the arena, and the public relations problems will effect stock prices and new business prospects. Such dilemmas are gathering in the wings.

Despite these anxieties, the growth of digital media, and the power of its marketing and political influence, may delay sensible restraints. Google and Facebook reportedly control more than 75% of online advertising revenue. Public affairs journalism in the context of social media, privately controlled, will continue to be an unfinished venture—by its very nature uncertain that it has the right answers. What it may, and should, depend upon is trying always to find the truth, which has more places to hide these days in the thickets of digital expression and its gigantic circulations.

There has never before been a private enterprise in America that can engage so many people, in such a multi-leveled manner, as the online platforms. The influence of their operations over daily life—social and business—is large enough to effect decisions and produce consequences of great significance in public affairs. Among them are unexpected consequences, and recommended actions, that might help or hurt whole segments of the population—with and without their consent. How some kind of restraint, or control, can be put in place to avoid harm will be the subject of debate and controversy in the years ahead.

Alexander Meiklejohn has the last word, "The freedom that the First Amendment provides is not, then, an absence of regulation. It is the presence of self-government."

14

Who is Watching the Watchdog?

FREEDOM OF THE press in America's earliest years was thought to be primarily a defense against government rather than a platform for individual expression. During the colonial years—more than a century—the British governors were a target of journalistic scrutiny, and they resented it. Their hostile reactions helped launch the movement towards American independence.

As a watchdog over government excess the press had to deal with sedition charges and reprisals against the publishers. The friction between newspapers and those in authority was part of American history, but disciplining the press without diminishing its freedom was an issue that would not go away. Could publishers regulate themselves? Collectively the proprietors seemed reluctant to collaborate except in regard to any encroachment on their freedom, either editorially or commercially. Adapting responsible restraints on sensationalism, obscenity, or incitement to violence were often discussed but rarely achieved consensus.

The Founders were, by and large, educated men who had some knowledge of the origins of democracy, particularly in ancient Greece. Giving the most humble citizen the right to vote allowed the Greek idea of a "sovereign people" to become a possibility. That idea was, many centuries later, central to America's "exceptionalism." Though it has never been fully realized, the concept of a sovereign people still seeks its place in the American dream, impeded as always by the barriers of ethnic rivalries, commercial interests, the influence of campaign financing, gerrymandering, and voter suppression. It has been supported, on the other hand, by a determined and at least partially independent press. An informed electorate may not be quite sovereign, but it finds its voice through public communication—once a handful of small circulation newspapers passed around at churches and taverns, and read aloud in family sitting rooms—now a horde of clamorous mass communication mechanisms ranging from print to video to digital that reach a potential audience of billions, not all of them voters and many uneducated.

The use of propaganda and falsity in the news media, along with the manipulation of facts, began with the first stirrings of political life in the ancient world. It was Aristotle who most eloquently advocated the "consent of the governed." That simple idea had provided Pericles, in the fifth century B.C., the opportunity to be elected fifteen times. Aristotle also recognized the importance of a strong middle class as opposed to a nation divided between oligarchs and impoverished peasants.

Most of those who came to embrace democratic principles of governance realized that information gave them power and that in a democracy information must be available to all—not only to the upper classes. Ancient Athens, for a while, provided access to the legislatures and courts

The use of propaganda and falsity in the news media, along with the manipulation of facts, began with the first stirrings of political life in the ancient world.

where the citizenry could watch and listen—a kind of real-time journalism, bearing witness to the events and the decisions of the day. That tradition resonated in the making of the United States Constitution and most fundamentally in the Bill of Rights.

Thomas Jefferson famously allowed that given a choice of government or newspapers he would prefer the papers—providing that every citizen received a copy and was capable of reading it.

The problems identified by access to information included public education, accurate reporting, and the wide distribution of the truth. In those days, and ever since, the truth was never simple or pure. It was, and remains, an aspiration—as John Stuart Mill would tell us—and that search must be illuminated by a free and responsible press. The message here is not complicated, not even elusive. Anyone who has found a "reliable source" can tell you that whatever we know that comes close to the truth has come from a reliable source. It does not appear everywhere. It requires effort and commitment. And it rarely pleases everyone.

Thomas Jefferson famously allowed that given a choice of government or newspapers he would prefer the papers— providing that every citizen received a copy and was capable of reading it.

Criticism of the press has come from many kinds of people—victims, adversaries, ideologues, scholars and well-informed observers. The best print and television reporting is produced by dedicated and well-prepared practitioners who are far less inclined to be biased than the average consumer of news. We all carry some baggage created by experience, but if the reporter allows personal feelings of disappointment or fear or venality to color his or her judgment, he or she will not earn the respect and trust of either audiences or colleagues.

Truth telling and intellectual honesty do not assure popularity, but they help form the best long-term reputations. Inevitably, and historically, the imagery of a watchdog has been attached to the practice of journalism. That function was part of the evolution of political analysis since the colonial years, and equally a part of the exasperation felt by public officials and institutional leaders. There have always been apprehensions regarding both the bark and the bite of the watchdog. This nuance triggered the logical but often petulant question: Who is watching the watchdog? Put another way, who or what can keep the press honest?

In the formative days of newspapers most of the readers knew who owned the papers. They were frequently controlled locally by individual politicians. When advertising revenue began to grow the issue shifted to the editorial influence of key advertisers. There is little disagreement about events and actions that should, or should not, go into the pages of mass communication instruments, or on the television screen, but news organizations reject any policing of their work. Among all the conferences and written reports on press ethics there is virtual unanimity concerning regulation of any kind beyond existing statutes, or commonly accepted obligation to be accurate—and within bounds on foul language and obscenity.

In theory, most news organizations subscribe to "self-regulation," but in practice the watchers of the watchdogs believe more is needed. Two possibilities have been seriously considered and occasionally employed—a monitoring body of some kind, and written codes. Overarching standards could be set for the digital media by a new statute—in effect a second "First Amendment" to cope with the electronic penetration achieved by planned misinformation, and technologies such as "chatbots."

The 1947 report written by the Commission on Freedom of the Press, discussed earlier, addressed the role and conduct of news organizations philosophically and existentially. In its statement of principle, Robert Hutchins wrote: "Freedom of speech and press is close to the central meaning of all liberty. When men cannot freely convey their thoughts to one another, no other liberty is secure."

James Madison had uttered almost the same words during the debates about the Bill of Rights in the late 1780s. He proclaimed a free press as "a sentinel over all our other liberties." The conduct and ethical standards of small newspapers were not the chief concern. Adjustments were more conveniently made in a time when circulations of individual papers were only in the hundreds, and the proprietors were widely known. The leap from a four-page "gazette" to Twitter is so great that Marshall McLuhan's insight—the medium is the message—not only materializes, but it suggests a new kind of communication far afield from traditional common values. Bringing the ethical perceptions of American democracy, with its reverence for individual rights, into the environment of digital immediacy and astronomical circulation, may be unmanageable. Applying legal or economic pressures to achieve ethical goals seems more realistic.

The legal route such as prosecution for "actual malice," or reckless disregard of the facts, requires little more than effectively using statutes already in place. What seems to be necessary now are new statutes that might control irresponsible electronic news media aggressively. If the various commercial platforms such as Google, Facebook, Microsoft et. al., can invoke legal measures allowing them to discipline offensive groups (or individual actors)—who create the editorial materials of fake news and other perversions of journalism—perhaps justifiable commercial restraints can be established that will have the muscle to discourage abuse of free expression in the digital forum.

One area that may welcome this kind of effort is the national security apparatus. Much of the anti-press commentary—political and patriotic—comes from

Bringing the ethical perceptions of American democracy, with its reverence for individual rights, into the environment of digital immediacy and astronomical circulation, may be unmanageable.

those who believe (or abuse) the notion that the press is not above the law, and terrorism is not protected by the First Amendment. In this context there has been a longstanding debate on the difference between informing the electorate and the danger of revealing vital security information to a lawless enemy.

Never in American history have the people in the enterprise called the free press faced such complicated and fateful issues of moral responsibility. To apply traditional ethical judgment to the instant availability of information purposefully delivered to millions of people is daunting, and the process cannot count on reflection or patience among the competitors. It takes only one mistake made in haste to cause considerable damage to defense and counterterrorism strategies. What is also part of the calculation is the ease with which sabotage by misinformation and falsification can be circulated widely to mislead and disrupt.

It is unlikely that restraint and verification will be an adequate response to openly provocative, let alone subtle and seemingly harmless, misinformation. The character and motivation of news organizations will always be a factor in combating the intentions of those who seek to harm a community, or a nation, that wishes to live in safety while still preserving its civil rights. The press must act as the voice of both protection for

In this context there has been a longstanding debate on the difference between informing the electorate and the danger of revealing vital security information to a lawless enemy.

the rights of a free society, and the security measures necessary to keep that society safe. Defining the line between them has entered the unfamiliar territory of technical knowledge and moral judgment. The game changer is the Internet which has altered journalism irrevocably.

Media commentator Nicholas Carr put it this way: "The most revolutionary consequence of the expansion of the Internet's power, scope and usefulness may not be that computers will start to think like us but that we will come to think like computers.... The artificial intelligence we are creating may turn out to be our own."

What can we do about all this? We have long-standing laws regarding harmful expression. We have the restraint that privately owned corporations in the communications business can bring to bear on wrong-doers. We also have the capacity to create new laws that deal with new technologies. Perhaps we may develop the resolve to form the independent monitoring entities—the think tanks and commissions that can advise and recommend the reforms and the remedies for unacceptable practices. In the environment of genuine innovation and entrepreneurial drive the counsel of experienced, knowledgeable men and women working in the public interest—with no disqualifying political or commercial connections—will be critical.

A century ago, by harnessing electricity, we were able to use technology to enhance and enlarge our physical capabilities. Now we are in a time when technology can increase our intellectual achievements by providing resources such as the Internet. The key question has been asked for decades—Who will be in charge, mankind or machines? It is doubtful that either can be a great success if the other is a failure.

15

The Human-Chip

VERY FEW COMMENTATORS who visited America in the 19th Century failed to report on the passion for news among the citizens of the young nation called the United States. They observed that newspapers were a vital part of daily life in the small towns and the expanding cities scattered from New England to the deep South. Alexis de Tocqueville, on his tour of America in 1831-32, described a "nation of conquerors who ... shut themselves in the American solitudes with an axe and some newspapers."

What was most remarkable about the hunger for news was the intense curiosity about public affairs. Government policies and political maneuvering engaged even the people who were not eligible to vote—the poor, women, blacks, Asians and American Indians among them.

For more than a century that yearning for information in America —information about politics and commerce in a new nation enlarging in both territorial size and population—was available in hundreds, eventually thousands, of small newspapers—discussed in earlier essays. There were no other choices to consider. News was not distributed in any other manner except for word of mouth, and those words themselves usually were drawn from the pages of a newspaper. Such a small resource was highly valued by the consumers, but publishers suffered many failures. Advertising revenue became essential, but it was not large enough to create economic security until the late 19th Century when circulations—particularly in urban centers—grew to a level that justified profitable rates.

Ironically there were never enough copies printed to permit per capita distribution, even in the early days when literate consumers were few in number. Each paper was passed around, and men who lived in rural farming communities would mount their horses and gallop into the nearest town to get the news and hurry back to their homes to tell their families. Acquiring a printed copy was not assured. An English visitor during the Jefferson Administration wrote home that "Men, women and children scampered up the road when they heard the coachman's horn begging for their favorite papers."

Foreign visitors were impressed by the fact that the diffusion of knowledge among the lower classes "by those who had been accustomed to homage and submission from their inferiors," as one British writer put it, was a good thing. The press was opening up the government to a much wider debate than Europeans could claim. In the United States, the taverns and the post offices became platforms for democratic discussion.

The profit motive also arrived with the coachman. As the newspapers tried to keep pace with urban growth, circulation and advertising gradually brought in substantial income. Journalism as a business matured and flourished. Technology altered the printing of news by introducing better means of reproduction, higher quality paper and ink, illustrations, photographs and color.

In little more than two centuries the distribution of information transformed the manner of its delivery into an electronic digital wonderland where news, and its tributaries, could be acquired from small, shiny devices in the palm of a human hand. The pace of change has been dazzling but certain imponderable issues for the reporting of news remained like stubborn passengers on a freight train. What can we believe, who can we trust, where is this taking us? So much of what we depend upon to live our lives, conduct our affairs, educate our children, maintain our safety, even entertain ourselves, is now mysteriously stored up in those shiny objects we hold in our hand, or on our laps.

The irascible journalist H.L. Mencken declared in the early 20th century: "What ails the newspapers of the United States is the fact that their gigantic commercial development compels them to appeal to larger and larger masses of undifferentiated men, and that truth is a commodity that the masses of undifferentiated men cannot be induced to buy."

The notion that truth can be bought and sold is a question the shiny objects cannot explain. As they assume greater control over what is still a human society, the micro-chip seems to be absorbing the human-chip, and not with much of a struggle. The struggle can be aroused by the human chip, but awakening human beings to that challenge is only possible if the level of education rises as rapidly as the dominance of technology.

The arrival of artificial intelligence and the use of computerized robots to perform more of what human beings have done for centuries will add weight and wonder to the conflict. The impact on information systems, including news, will be critical. The computer has already been added to the production line of newspapers, magazines and books. Electronic tools provide research, design, and the rendering of words on paper and online. What has not been provided by mechanical means is elegance, empathy, humor or wisdom—to name a few qualities that, for the time being, remain part of a living human sensibility.

As they assume greater control over what is still a human society, the micro-chip seems to be absorbing the human-chip, and not with much of a struggle.

Embedded in that sensibility is a moral imagination. It stimulates the judgment and the compassion that a machine cannot yet produce. The information in specific terms may be programmed into artificial intelligence, but the impulse to create the ideas remains intrinsically and exclusively human. Can a machine independently perform the thinking, the emotional responses, and the subtlety required to make the choices that have always separated human beings from all other creatures? If machines can provide such creativity independently, human beings will—or at least can—fall under the mechanical power and ingenuity of those machines which are presumably more efficient and indefatigable than the human mind. What would be the consequences of that development? Will a few supremely talented human beings question the need for other human beings?

Technology could influence the patterns of human behavior. The workforce will need to prepare for different tasks than are now commonly anticipated. The nature of education will shift its focus and its methodologies. Intellectual ambitions will demand databases and search engines astonishingly more comprehensive and swift than what is currently available. Research will move us towards knowledge and discovery at a pace that seems unfathomable. And explaining all these developments will become part of the daily news. Reporting and analyzing that news and incorporating it into self-governance—indeed into whatever form democracy may take—will become more scientific in process, but still in need of a fundamental moral compass, as it has been since the dawn of language. Communications of facts and opinions, ideas and policies, inspiration and critical reasoning, will not be machine-made. If they are, it will be because humanity surrenders the meaning of life to technology.

Dialogue between those who welcome technology wherever it arises, and those who fear its effects on civilized societies, has been impassioned and provocative. Stephen Hawking, a great physicist and public intellectual, said not long before his death in 2018,

> "If machines produce everything we need, the outcome will depend on how things are distributed. Everyone can enjoy a life of luxurious leisure if the machine-produced wealth is shared, or most people can end up miserably poor if the machine owners successfully lobby against wealth distribution. So far, the trend seems to be toward the second option, with technology driving ever increasing inequality."

Hawking's admonishment points to the possibility of enlightened government actions worldwide that might control the extension of artificial intelligence in a manner that would not deter the progress of science, but could prevent the uncontrollable growth of unemployment brought on by automation.

In regard to communication of public affairs there have been interesting experiments and much speculation. As noted earlier, in the 1960s an English professor at the University of Toronto, named Marshall McLuhan, introduced an entirely different view of media. He believed that the medium used to communicate ideas and information seriously—sometimes critically—shaped the content of the communication. Charles Van Doren in his book "A History of Knowledge: Past, Present, and Future" sees McLuhan as one of the most important figures in 20th century intellectual development.

McLuhan classified communication into three groups— oral, print, and electronic. For example, a story printed on paper was not received the same way as the story produced on a television screen. Lewis Mumford, in the 1970s, wrote a multi-volume book called "The Myth of the Machine" in which he rejected the idea that technology determines the "course of history." His fear was that Western society is inclined to constantly "create technological novelties, but equally the duty to surrender to these novelties unconditionally."

As noted earlier, in the 1960s an English professor at the University of Toronto, named Marshall McLuhan, introduced an entirely different view of media.

Mumford advocated that technology should not control us. We should control technology. The human mind, he believed, must take command over the machine it creates. Nicholas Carr remonstrates with Mumford. He doesn't accept that technology becomes a duty. He sees it as the "consequence of economic forces that lie largely beyond our control." Carr asserts that technology has progressed because of its demonstrable influence "on the cost of producing and comparing goods and services."

Taken in the context of communication the economic issues remain largely the same and the conversation is lively. Oral traditions gave way to the printing press, and the news business then confronted the growth of television. McLuhan's maxim that the medium is the message is still relevant. The digital technology that seemed for a while to be a parallel universe soon intersected with traditional communications. Going online was not just an option. It became an imperative.

The transition brings with it the destructive power of disinformation, falsehoods massively disseminated, and the omnipresent, deliberate erosion of truth. The press institutionally can confront the loss of trust that follows misuse of technology by setting ethical standards for news reporting and the major communications platforms. This is a moral issue that will trouble all our institutions for years to come. The exercise of due diligence, as always, will be vital. Technology as a creative force fears regulation for obvious reasons—not least the stifling of innovation. But due diligence must find a way of giving space to invention and progress while protecting the public interest.

> *The digital technology that seemed for a while to be a parallel universe soon intersected with traditional communications. Going online was not just an option. It became an imperative.*

As the *New York Times* wryly reported, in addition to giving journalists more time to pursue their interests, the use of AI programs comes with an added benefit for editors. "One thing I've noticed," an editor observed, "is that our AI written articles have zero typos." The News Guild of New York, an organization that watches over employment issues, has indicated that they are monitoring emerging technologies to make sure that jobs are not being threatened by machines. Francesco Marconi, the head of research and development at the *Wall Street Journal*, says AI "gives you more access, and you get more information quicker, but it is a new field and technology changes. Today it's AI, tomorrow it's blockchain, and in ten years it will be something else. What does not change is the journalistic standard."

16

———

Looking Forward

THE SOCIAL CONTEXT created by digital technology has transformed reality for many institutions and commercial enterprises. The effect on what is called the news business is visible, audible, and profoundly unsettling. The large distribution platforms like Twitter, Facebook, Google, et al., have become so essential in the lives of millions of people that any interruption in their services has severe, even traumatic, consequences—economically, politically, psychologically. The anxiety stimulated by dependence on digital instruments is understandable—often underestimated.

Imminent developments include the power of "artificial intelligence." David Gelertner, a professor of computer science at Yale University, explored its potential impact in his book called "The Tides of Mind: Uncovering the Spectrum of Consciousness." Gelertner is convinced that scientists will develop a robot with human characteristics and eventually the capacity to "achieve humanlike thought." He agrees that computers will never *feel* anything but maintains that artificial intelligence can build a simulated mind that reproduces "all the nuances of human thought...despite being unconscious."

It should be noted here that Professor Gelertner is one of the distinguished thinkers about technology who received a letter-bomb in 1978 from a man named Theodore Kaczynski, known to the public as the Unabomber. It exploded in Gelertner's hands and left him permanently disabled.

> *He agrees that computers will never feel anything but maintains that Artificial Intelligence can build a simulated mind that reproduces "all the nuances of human thought... despite being unconscious."*

Kaczynski was obsessively opposed to the prospects of technology becoming so essential that human beings would find themselves inescapably dependent on it. He devised bombs that would fit into envelopes and small packages sent to selected scientists who Kaczynski believed were central to the empowerment of machines.

From 1978 to 1995, twenty six scientists were injured, three of them fatally, by Kaczynski's devices. In 1998, from his unknown location in a forest cabin, he negotiated an exceptional agreement with the *New York Times* and the *Washington Post*. Both organizations agreed to publish a manifesto written by Kaczynski in return for his promise to end the bombing. The manifesto declared, in part, that machines were becoming "more and more intelligent" and "people will let machines make more of their decisions for them." The language of the manifesto convinced Kaczynski's older brother, and his mother, that he was surely the author. They decided they must notify the authorities, and with their help the FBI tracked him to his primitive hideaway, where he was arrested and eventually sent to prison.

Professor Gelertner and colleagues were not persuaded to give up their research. Of "super computers," Gelertner, in 2016, wrote: "They are all natural outcomes of the human need to build and understand. We can't shut that down and don't want to." Gelertner did repeat an earlier warning, "Let normal people beware of Artificial Intelligence researchers."

The lurking question is what would be the behavior of the "super robot" towards human beings? If it can act independently, might it turn on its creators? In regard to that possibility Professor Gelertner provides more cautionary words: "Thoughtful people everywhere ought to resolve that it would be unspeakably stupid to allow technologists to fool around with human-like and super-human machines—except with the whole world's intense scrutiny."

The most likely scrutinizer is a free and responsible press. Meanwhile the Internet can amplify all kinds of human evils—falsehoods, incitements, bigotry and hate. The major distribution companies have already begun an organized effort to deny the worst of human endeavors a place on the Internet. But those who have studied the threat of hate organizations wonder if there is not a need for new statutes and regulations that can deal with the size and speed of the Internet, much as statutes and regulations have already placed some institutional restraints on television, cable and print media.

Germany, where during the 1930s hatred was nationalized in a country believed to be the most advanced culture in Europe, has worked steadily since World War II at establishing the strongest barriers against bigotry and hate in the Western world. Germany now has laws that forbid even the most feeble steps towards a revival of the Nazi atrocities. Such measures may be inadequate as so many countries are moving politically towards radical populism.

Some Americans feel we do not need encumbrances on the First Amendment, but no one has come up with an effective means of preventing the harm—individual or collective—that online fabrications and contrived distortions can inflict, almost instantaneously, on the lives of innocent people. This has been done repetitively and so persuasively that truth cannot correct the narrative before blatant lies become accepted by large segments of the population.

The recruiting of members by such groups as ISIS internationally, and white nationalists domestically, has been carried out online with visual materials and seductive soundtracks that are disconcertingly clever and professional. The traditional style of news reporting on public and private affairs has been utilized by extremist recruiters directly and indirectly. Demonizing the mainline, or "elite," media is part of the message.

What is now clear is the fact that the Internet provides an opportunity for the promulgation of a kind of "siren song" which is especially attractive to resentful, discontented young people who enter the combative world of organizations like ISIS, white supremacists, neo-Nazis, or the Ku Klux Klan. The electronic systems promotes the allure of "virtual communities" that the news media does not provide. The psychology of Internet recruitment video can be so powerful, at its best, that countervailing action on the

The traditional style of news reporting on public and private affairs has been utilized by extremist recruiters directly and indirectly.

part of free and open societies seems critically necessary. The idea that First Amendment freedoms of expression protect the right of adversaries to plant the seeds of destruction of those very same freedoms is possible and deeply troubling.

Since the founding of the United States and the ratification of a Bill of Rights, protecting the speech we detest as vigorously as the sentiments we love, has been part of the American experience. Disingenuous defenders of the Constitution have complained about, and some have tried to eliminate, the expression of ideas they may not like—rationalizing that such ideas will subvert the principles of the Constitution and its amendments. Almost always, attempts to silence the words we do not approve of—some of them incontrovertibly ugly or offensive—have been rejected by the courts because of First Amendment protections. Other advocates of free expression have declared that better words, corrective facts, and debate and dissent in the "marketplace of ideas," would inevitably enlighten a freedom-loving populace, who over time would condemn the offensive, the hateful, or any anti-American activity of misguided or malevolent groups, as unacceptable.

The idea that First Amendment freedoms of expression protect the right of adversaries to plant the seeds of destruction of those very same freedoms is possible and deeply troubling.

That has sometimes been the outcome, but technology has now given the forces of evil and violence a facility to make their case so mesmerically, so swiftly, and so widely that a hostile, destructive purpose is realized before contradiction can be heard. A new agenda of unabashed propaganda—misinformation, distortion, outright falsehoods—threatens to reduce the First Amendment to a frail and powerless anachronism. That raises a crucial question. How does a free society legally protect its constitutional freedoms against those who would destroy them by using the Constitution itself as a license?

17

―――

Due Diligence,
the Critical Element

HEREWITH, SOME SUGGESTIONS for remedial action. These thoughts are in effect a reflection on the preceding essays in one sense, but hopefully a fresh calculation in another.

The range of freedom of expression has often included innuendo, sarcasm and insult, which could easily spill into slander and libel. Legal response to such offensiveness is usually painful and expensive.

American newspapers historically could match the venom of any outspoken publication in the world. Agreeing on some standards of civility was not a priority. The attempt to define and practice ethical principles remains a challenge for news organizations. However, the need for trust and respect has never been so great as in the current technological ferment.

There is, especially in these times, the pervasive issue of managing the use of the Internet. Mass circulation newspapers and magazines, radio and television, have traditionally faced charges of abusing freedom of expression—many times over many years—but the courts have been able to settle most of the conflicts. Nonetheless the legal fees are sometimes so large that presumably innocent parties cannot risk the possibility of losing a lawsuit. Some have had to go out of business. The idea that financially secure media companies can intimidate smaller, vulnerable competitors by threatening long, costly litigation is unjust and contrary to the spirit of the Constitution—but that does not necessarily protect the innocent.

Dealing with the immediate abuse of power is possible for some well-funded individuals and organizations. Others must suffer unreasonably. The Internet impact is formidable in ways that actually create an entirely new dynamic territory—one that is so compelling and far-reaching that it seems to call for a kind of surveillance and restraint never considered before.

During the 2016 political campaign, the use (and abuse) of social media demonstrated a particularly corrosive problem for our democracy. The Trump campaign was not alone in using meticulously selected Internet materials, but it did so more extensively than any other political organization, and it identified and targeted like-minded groups advantageously. In a *New Yorker* article in 2017, writer Adrian Chen produced a disturbing analysis of how truth suffered in the campaign for the American presidency during 2016. Chen documents

the manipulation of social media by unidentified propaganda and misinformation experts. He acknowledges that this is not the first time political planning included deliberate misinformation, but the volume of 2016 activity had never been seen before. U.S. intelligence agents found that a targeted mass of 126 million potential voters were reached with deceptive, fake information. The attempt to influence elections here (and in Europe) was spear-

The Trump campaign was not alone in using meticulously selected Internet materials, but it did so more extensively than any other political organization, and it identified and targeted like-minded groups advantageously.

headed by Russian "trolls" who were ushering in a `post-truth' Internet world where people based their opinions not on facts or reason, but on passion and prejudice.

Overwhelmingly, pro-Trump messages of so-called "fake news" were compounded by "this sense that the role of the press had been ceded to an arcane algorithmic system created by private companies that are only about the bottom line."

Equally important was the fact that democratic institutions, traditionally able to hold back outright lies and malevolence, were weakened and fragmented in a manner both unanticipated and surprisingly effective. The erosion of respect for fact-based evidence, and the acceptance of falsehoods by so many voters, leaves the responsible communication companies, the government, and concerned citizens in confusion and doubt. It also leaves the door open to extremist populism. As new elections approached, the FBI, among other agencies, persistently warned that the door was still ajar.

At right (page 157) is a page from from the Mueller Report summarizing interventions in our 2016 election.

Equally important was the fact that democratic institutions, traditionally able to hold back outright lies and malevolence, were weakened and fragmented in a manner both unanticipated and surprisingly effective.

Similar use of misinformation is still being attributed by American intelligence agencies to Russian operatives, and their associates in America. They fed fabrications into the Internet's distribution systems discrediting Mrs. Clinton, and praising Mr. Trump, in the weeks before the election, with an emphasis on key states that could determine the Electoral College outcome. Despite the fact that Mrs. Clinton had very close to three million more votes nationally, she lost the Electoral College. Many Americans are asking when will we address—or prevent—the distortions of the Electoral College.

There is a fundamental disconnect in the fact that the information available on the Internet can be wrong—by omission, by deliberate falsehood, or by miscalculation. No remedy is infallible, but like the spirit and letter of the rule of law in any other sector, law and legislation can be called upon in that context—without violating the profound importance of the

U.S. Department of Justice
~~Attorney Work Product // May Contain Material Protected Under Fed. R. Crim. P. 6(e)~~

EXECUTIVE SUMMARY TO VOLUME I

RUSSIAN SOCIAL MEDIA CAMPAIGN

The Internet Research Agency (IRA) carried out the earliest Russian interference operations identified by the investigation—a social media campaign designed to provoke and amplify political and social discord in the United States. The IRA was based in St. Petersburg, Russia, and received funding from Russian oligarch Yevgeniy Prigozhin and companies he controlled. Prigozhin is widely reported to have ties to Russian President Vladimir Putin, Harm to Ongoing Matter

In mid-2014, the IRA sent employees to the United States on an intelligence-gathering mission with instructions Harm to Ongoing Matter

The IRA later used social media accounts and interest groups to sow discord in the U.S. political system through what it termed "information warfare." The campaign evolved from a generalized program designed in 2014 and 2015 to undermine the U.S. electoral system, to a targeted operation that by early 2016 favored candidate Trump and disparaged candidate Clinton. The IRA's operation also included the purchase of political advertisements on social media in the names of U.S. persons and entities, as well as the staging of political rallies inside the United States. To organize those rallies, IRA employees posed as U.S. grassroots entities and persons and made contact with Trump supporters and Trump Campaign officials in the United States. The investigation did not identify evidence that any U.S. persons conspired or coordinated with the IRA. Section II of this report details the Office's investigation of the Russian social media campaign.

RUSSIAN HACKING OPERATIONS

At the same time that the IRA operation began to focus on supporting candidate Trump in early 2016, the Russian government employed a second form of interference: cyber intrusions (hacking) and releases of hacked materials damaging to the Clinton Campaign. The Russian intelligence service known as the Main Intelligence Directorate of the General Staff of the Russian Army (GRU) carried out these operations.

In March 2016, the GRU began hacking the email accounts of Clinton Campaign volunteers and employees, including campaign chairman John Podesta. In April 2016, the GRU hacked into the computer networks of the Democratic Congressional Campaign Committee (DCCC) and the Democratic National Committee (DNC). The GRU stole hundreds of thousands of documents from the compromised email accounts and networks. Around the time that the DNC announced in mid-June 2016 the Russian government's role in hacking its network, the GRU began disseminating stolen materials through the fictitious online personas "DCLeaks" and "Guccifer 2.0." The GRU later released additional materials through the organization WikiLeaks.

freedom of expression.

To begin with, there are laws, regulations, traditions and ethical standards already part of American institutional and intellectual life. Yale Law Professor Akhil Reed Amar, author of several acclaimed books on the Constitution, writes: "America's *unwritten* Constitution encompasses not only rules specifying the substantive content of the nation's supreme law but also rules clarifying the methods for determining the meaning of this supreme law."

All of this inevitably depends upon the support of responsible citizens. In the operation of the Internet platforms we are, more often than not, dealing with proprietors and executives of private enterprises. The Constitution presides over these enterprises as if they are citizens. They must abide by the laws of the land, and they must understand in addition the statutes and commonly accepted standards governing commercial activity.

Because the Internet provides news and public affairs information, the First Amendment is particularly relevant. That connection means that libel, slander, hate speech, and false advertising, among other charges, can become a reality whenever the Internet is used—or misused—by people with an illicit agenda, or hateful ideologies such as racism. Some laws are already in place, but the cost of employing them is beyond the average citizen's reach, and the time it takes to secure some kind of justice can be self-defeating. There is no justice after falsehoods or bigotry have been promulgated online, purposefully and deceptively, in a manner that reaches millions of consumers nationally—and internationally. Justice requires *early prevention* in the digital universe. And that is a serious aspect of the current news environment, different from what we've known and understood throughout our history until now.

Prevention means stopping the distribution of libel and lies and hate before they are widely seen and heard and read—not *after* the damage is done and cannot be repaired. Over time, if the existing laws are not adequate, there may be a need for new laws.

In recent years, First Amendment jurisprudence aspired to protect American citizens from *false* information, *actual* libel, and *reckless* disregard of the facts while managing to keep the door open to robust debate, candor, and passion. The US

> *Prevention means stopping the distribution of libel and lies and hate before they are widely seen and heard and read— not* after *the damage is done and cannot be repaired.*

Supreme Court, in effect, protected public criticism of government officials—providing such commentary was not *knowingly false.* The Court reiterated that "robust" debate was vital to democracy and would be difficult—or impossible—if the participants had to be certain that every word was factually correct. One consequence has been "self-censorship," which has inevitably silenced much dissent as well as truth.

Not surprisingly democracy has required a fair measure of

good will among those who participate—in the conception and implementation of principles; in the administration of justice; in the enlargement or limitation of impact or influence. In all these possible developments the form of government and the kind of society produced by the idea called "democracy" needs people of good will. The integrity and sensibility of governance without good will on all sides invites both corruption and mismanagement.

The Court reiterated that "robust" debate was vital to democracy and would be difficult—or impossible—if the participants had to be certain that every word was factually correct.

Good will is not defined in simple terms, but it represents the ethical perception and strength of a reasonably informed society. Thoughtful, educated men and women know how important respect and civility are to our democratic traditions. A mutual regard for "doing the right thing" means, for instance, caring for the least fortunate, and the disabled—to say nothing of those who are voiceless.

James Madison in the Federalist Papers wrote about citizens willing to serve the public good: "…there is a degree of depravity in mankind which requires a certain degree of circumspection and distrust, so there are other qualities in human nature which justify a certain portion of esteem and confidence." Madison found the better qualities in adequate supply to assure "sufficient virtue among men for self-government." What would he find today?

These are not foolish expectations, but in the 21st Century they may be unrealistic. Virtue will not automatically triumph over "fake news," "alternate facts" and the enormous power of the Internet to distribute malevolence. The fundamental issue is that truth is no longer a definable entity in our lives. The meaning of truth has been subjected to so many manipulations that it has become irrelevant to large segments of the population who prefer some version of their own presuppositions.

Christopher Lasch in his classic 1978 book, "The Culture of Narcissism," cites the remarks of Richard Nixon's press secretary, Ron Ziegler, who admitted in 1974 that his previous statements on Watergate had become "inoperative." Some in his audience thought he was trying to say that he had lied. "What he meant," Lasch wrote, "was that his earlier statements were no longer believable. Not their

> *Virtue will not automatically triumph over "fake news," "alternate facts" and the enormous power of the Internet to distribute malevolence.*

falsity but their reliability to command assent rendered them 'inoperative.' The question of whether they were *true* or not was beside the point."

Consider that Lasch was making these observations before the arrival of the Internet. The same perception can, of course, be made today—any day, any hour—in the digital era, but its effects are alarmingly swifter and more widespread than Lasch might have expected—no matter how prophetic he was.

That is the issue—the size and transformational nature of the information machinery. The Internet can produce its "virtual communities" based on a dazzling array of "untruth," given credibility by technology. So-called "alternate facts"— usually fictional—may sound authentic when actually devoid of authenticity. The current efforts to somehow prevent malicious falsehoods to be promulgated online poses the seemingly unrealistic notion of asking private companies to censor themselves—or at least reject material they believe is false, dangerous, hateful (among other unacceptable characteristics). The alternative is surrendering the disciplinary function to government authorities, or to independent organizations devoted to the public interest.

The best arrangement might well be a non-governmental group of distinguished, qualified men and women from the appropriate professional communities, including such organizations as the Pulitzer Prize Board, the Nieman Fellowship, academic societies, journalists, and corporate executives. The carefully selected cohort of experienced practitioners could form the necessary committees that would provide guidance and standards for the major corporations that own the platforms through which most of the news and general information is distributed to more than one third of the human race—particularly to the segment known as "educated people."

They could establish, as already discussed, which companies had earned formal recognition for integrity and ethical responsibility. Such recognition would be renewed at least annually, not unlike FCC or SEC approval, but presumably after thorough reviews that would provide credentials, and approve rejections of materials not acceptable for distribution on the Internet. They would also recommend fines for violations like those now being imposed in Germany and other European countries—and in China—when companies are not in compliance with the existing rules or too slow in taking down unacceptable data, fake news and fabrications.

Whatever the manner of financing and administrating this group—let us call it an Advisory Board—and the authority given to it would have to be convincing, along with the firmly established obligation of the participating corporations to abide by membership requirements.

There are many such structures in American business and professional life. This one would protect the information platforms and their very large body of consumers—domestic and international—on many levels. Perhaps the agreements between the groups could free presumably independent corporations from the complex task of determining what material should not be allowed to appear on their information platforms.

The radically changed universe of communication has already encountered and altered reality. Preserving the values and freedoms of the news media demands equally large adjustments in how we construct a framework of self-man-agement, and the role of government. Due diligence will be necessary. As previously noted in these pages, due diligence calls on the individual citizens to find for themselves the best means of verifying the information they receive, and iden-tifying the media they can trust. There are fact-check-ing services such as *Snopes*, *Factcheck.org* and *Politifact* already in place. There will surely be others, but the art of verification will develop primarily because of the great need for it. The process and the individual responsi-bility must move together in the current atmosphere of a "precocious devotion to untruth."

Perhaps the agreements between the groups could free presumably independent corporations from the complex task of determining what material should not be allowed to appear on their information platforms.

America long ago took its free press for granted. That luxury is no longer possible. The next few decades will see many struggles to set the standards for First Amendment regulations that can accommodate the expansive technology gathering around information and news.

Unless we can protect truth and its reliability the forces of ignorance and distortion that occupy so many information sites will erode the progress we call civilization. In the United States especially, where the dignity of the individual has been a hallmark of a "Great Experiment," the deep-running princi-ples of a free and responsible press have to be nurtured and burnished steadily and transparently to prevent the misuse of a technology that is of our own making.

The most insidious threat to freedom now is the ease with which cynical, dishonest people have successfully tried to render truth irrelevant by distributing lies and deceptions so widely and frequently. Nonetheless, Senator Moynihan's Doctrine endures: "Everyone is entitled to his own opinion, but not his own facts."

Historian Timothy Snyder in his book *On Tyranny*, urges us to believe in truth. "To abandon facts," he writes, "is to abandon freedom. If nothing is true, then no one can criticize power, because there is no basis on which to do it."

Whatever else you might take away from these essays, I hope you will remember how important it is to search for truth in a world that is discovering its absence. The truth that makes justice possible, the truth that makes our country confident, and the truth that illuminates the Constitution is vital to a healthy democracy. A nation without reliable facts, and therefore without trust in itself, is doomed to failure.

In the coming years the news media will face a continuing obligation to manage print, television and Internet delivery systems. The fragmentation of news has been in itself a problem that shapes public opinion and the voting process. Technological change has been a significant factor in the evolution of news reporting throughout American history, but the advent of computer science, social media and artificial intelligence has altered the nature of news so dramatically that fundamental values are in peril.

Seeking the truth, verifying facts based on evidence, rendering information with fairness and accuracy, are qualifications that now become more vulnerable to manipulation and deception. The ability of special interests—including foreign powers—to invade the Internet platforms, and distort the messages that reach millions of voters, has infected free expression with carefully constructed falsehoods and propaganda. This destructive use of technology, targeted and well-researched, engages audiences shrewdly and repeatedly. How much it has moved election results in both 2016 and 2018—to say nothing of 2020—will be the subject of research and discovery for years to come.

Seeking the truth, verifying facts based on evidence, rendering information with fairness and accuracy, are qualifications that now become more vulnerable to manipulation and deception.

The term "post-truth" is commonly used. Millions of people appear to be willing to accept whatever they are told by political figures they like, despite contradictions and inconsistencies. Due diligence and fact-checking need organized help from experts. The effort also needs sophisticated, experienced reporters who will find the best sources of corroboration (or lack of it), and will bring both education and intuition to the process.

Truth seeking, after all, is indeed a work in progress. It may require corrections, and it will always be cumulative. Deadlines are a way of saying, "This is what we know so far."

The most important factor, at the end of the day, is trust. If we don't trust our leaders—on either side of the issues, and if we don't trust the messengers who bring us the news, we cannot sustain a democracy. Ironically, in a time when computers and robots may be programmed to a level of skill superior to the performance of human beings, the question of democracy as the governing principle that is described in our Constitution will not be a meaningful concern. When automation and algorithms dominate, the individual, average citizen will have neither dignity nor importance.

18

The Collaborators

THE INDIVIDUAL CITIZEN will, in the view of the more apocalyptic scientists, depend upon computers and robots. The artificial intelligence devices of the future theoretically make most human beings unnecessary—economically, militarily and politically. The "system" will keep a few superhuman individuals in positions of influence—at least in the short run.

Max Tegmark is an MIT professor who has organized a grant program for AI safety research, along with Elon Musk who is best known for his development of electric cars. They encourage research based on four technical disciplines—verification, validation, security and control.

Verification, in Tegmark's view, asks "Did I build the system right?" *Validation* asks, "Did I build the right system?" *Security* involves protection against hackers and malicious software, known as "malware." *Control* requires a human monitor—or what many scientists call "human-in-the-loop."

There are many examples of vulnerabilities in artificial intelligence machine design, but airplane crashes during the first half of 2019 are the most notable. The Tegmark-Musk safety principles might have prevented such disasters, but Tegmark concludes, "In the ongoing computer security arms race between offense and defense, there is so far little indication that defense is winning." One possibility (already cited) that many scientists have discussed is the concept of an outside, independent group of experts who will supervise the process of rejecting inappropriate research. What is not yet clear is how eagerly the large communication companies will welcome independent judgments on content.

In 2014, Tegmark founded a nonprofit organization called "The Future of Life Institute." Its goal was to make people think about the fact that "Technology was giving life the power either to flourish like never before or to self-destruct." The first meeting of about 30 academics and students agreed that scientists must confront biotech, nuclear weapons, and climate change, but they also agreed "Our first major goal should be to help make AI safety research mainstream."

Tegmark then persuaded Stephen Hawking, Nobel Laureate Frank Wilczek and Stuart Russell to join him in composing an op-ed piece meant to arouse public interest in AI safety. Arianna Huffington placed it on the front page of the *Huffington Post,* and it stimulated wide coverage of the topic over the following year. Tegmark was not resting. With the help of several colleagues he persuaded a large group of scientists, scholars and corporate leaders to gather at a resort in Puerto Rico where they could meet free of any media coverage. Their discussion topic was "The Future of AI: Opportunities and Challenges." A surprising consensus emerged which was put into a public letter ultimately signed by more than 8,000 researchers and interested AI technologists. The letter called for a redefining of the goals of AI to "create not undirected intelligence, but beneficial intelligence."

The key point of the letter was the moral aspect of AI research, because it can effect the future of human life on this planet and beyond. The issues of scientific progress and the quality of life are integrated in the basic concerns of the text, including expectations and timeframe. An illustration in Tegmark's book is captioned: "It's at least decades away, but it may take that long to make it safe."

In Europe particularly, but in other parts of the world as well, AI scientists have pondered the moral challenges and, in many cases, begun the establish-

> *The key point of the letter was the moral aspect of AI research, because it can effect the future of human life on this planet and beyond.*

ment of cautionary measures—some of them referred to in earlier pages. There are small groups of scientists and public intellectuals already working on such matters as banning autonomous military weapons; delineating dangerous medical procedures; and conducting experiments that should be prohibited for the protection of human life from the misuse of artificial intelligence. For the moment, and probably for a long time to come, the scrutiny and courage of the news media will be the major safeguard. What is indisputable is the stark reality that within the realm of artificial intelligence and the eventual development of what is called "AGI"—Artificial General Intelligence—lies the potential power of destructive forces, both direct and uncontrollable, which need to be anticipated and dealt with before they happen. The future does not yet belong to machines and may never, but if it is going to belong to human beings we need to find a way to make greater sense out of the data flow that is inundating our daily lives, and we need to engage knowledgeable people the world over in that effort.

> *For the moment, and probably for a long time to come, the scrutiny and courage of the news media will be the major safeguard.*

Among the scientists working on the "learning machines" that have already entered the operations of industrial, military and medical organizations, are those who envision a dynamic collaboration of human intelligence and machine intelligence. They point to the programming of nearly autonomous computers, and the algorithms that instruct AI mechanical contrivances—all composed and installed by human beings. Whatever intellectual or scientific versatility is transferred to machines, the creativity and competence involved is man-made. These same human minds will in theory control their progeny, and will enhance the lives of all humans by harnessing and harvesting the computer's capacity and power to do the work of a healthy, rewarding existence.

These will include scientists who have led the way in creating "neural networks"—a term that could help describe a brain. The brain-like function in a computer has been explored for several decades. In effect, the neural network takes the "learning machine" closer to the "thinking machine."

Those who believe human ingenuity will one day—perhaps 30 years forward, perhaps a century—create the neural network that will produce consciousness in an AI machine, are already developing "deep-learning machines."

Among the scientists working on the "learning machines" that have already entered the operations of industrial, military and medical organizations, are those who envision a dynamic collaboration of human intelligence and machine intelligence.

The prestigious Turing Award, in 2018, went to three Canadians—Geoffrey Hinton, Yann LeCun, and Yoshua Bengio—for demonstrating that machines can learn like humans. Hinton was, and is, a pioneer in the field of neural networks. He has for many years been a leader in the journey AI is making towards a human level in most, if not all skills. The goal is to make something that functions like neurons, connected by synapses, as in the human brain. Our neurons—billions of them—are electro-chemical devices which seem to be able to signal one another both electrically and chemically, causing actions and functions we call "intelligence." Science has not yet fully discovered how the neurons operate, but computer scientists have learned how to simulate in neural networks the same activity as biological neurons.

In his book *Life 3.0*, Tegmark provides an explanation that the least knowledgeable of us may find useful—myself included. He writes: "...evolution probably didn't make our biological neurons so complicated because it was necessary, but because it was more efficient—and because evolution, as opposed to human engineers, doesn't reward designs that are simple and easy to understand."

> *Those who believe human ingenuity will one day—perhaps 30 years forward, perhaps a century—create the neural network that will produce consciousness in an AI machine, are already developing "deep-learning machines."*

We know that not all predictions of AI's destiny are optimistic, but the apprehensions are worth considering. People like Bill Gates, Elon Musk and Stephen Hawking cannot be dismissed. They, and others not so prominent, have expressed concerns about military activity, job loss, legal complexities, and the fate of human society. The segment of AI researchers, who doubt serious dangers will emerge in less than a century, worry that beneficial research and development will be hampered by the fear of risk. Paranoia can encourage unnecessary regulation. There is even a suspicion that "carbon-based" development is favored over "silicon-based" development. Phrases like "digital utopians" enter the discussions.

This is heady stuff—these potentials. Much is still theory and ambition. The machines—as we know—are not yet able to feel, to empathize, to be conscious. Meanwhile non-conscious intelligence can do many things that will change the world we live in. But, we continue to believe, only a conscious mind can produce compassion, ethical judgment, and independent action. In the movie "I, Robot" actor Will Smith challenged a robot by asking, "Can a robot write a symphony? Can a robot turn a canvas into a beautiful masterpiece?" The robot looks the human in the eye, somewhat winsomely, and asks, "Can *you?*"

Science will not go away. Machines will be made and programmed. Discoveries will alter the pace and the nature of artificial intelligence. A thinking machine is possible—especially to scientists. One day, they believe—perhaps not in this century—the machines will achieve consciousness and independence. Will there be a "Stop" button? Will someone pull the plug? Will human society and democracy survive?

These are realistic questions for those who have faith in the inevitable progress of artificial intelligence. The believers and the skeptics—and all those around them—will need a responsible, ethical press that will monitor and explain and stimulate the fundamental interests of a human society—not least in regard to the machines that human minds have conceived.

Will human beings be able to preserve a viable role on the planet Earth as the machines they have created and programmed become increasingly competent and autonomous?

Education may well produce new kinds of jobs for intelligent individuals, but vast unemployment among working class people is anticipated in any event. They will require some kind of safety net, funded possibly by the significant added wealth the artificial intelligence machines will create.

The believers and the skeptics— and all those around them—will need a responsible, ethical press that will monitor and explain and stimulate the fundamental interests of a human society.

But in the long run, many scientists believe the machines will progress inexorably toward new levels of autonomy and capacity provided by the algorithms of human programmers, and they will presumably become smarter than their inventors. If and when that happens, human minds will either find a way of collaborating with artificial intelligence or surrendering to it. We know that some of the scientists in the field believe a partnership is possible. Others consider it unavoidable that mankind must one day decide whether it wants to be "livestock or pets"—in a new world with unimaginable patterns of existence, and a planetary universe waiting in silence for legions of mechanized explorers.

Law scholars have provided ideas for adjusting the legal system—or creating special formulations—to deal with robots and algorithms. What has not been widely explored is how human society can control the nature and growth of artificial intelligence so that mankind can defend itself against obsolescence. Human beings, on a global basis, will need to agree on the kind of laws and regulations that will permit the restructuring of the workforce, and assure the cooperation of science and industry regarding the ethical management of data, and computational machines. Confronting unemployment (brought on by robots and AI), and open source Internet information, will require foresight, good will and constant due diligence—a thought that needs repeating.

Despite such challenges, human society, under the influence of enlightened and talented leadership, might engage with artificial intelligence in a "survival partnership." It is unlikely that science will stand still, and agreement between nations such as China and Russia, the European Union and the United States will not come obediently. Cooperation may not trump competition. The idea that hostile interests will secretly create robots they might not ultimately control—is the dark side of futuristic speculation. The echoes of fiction and films about evil machines attacking human beings murmur in the background. We are reminded of Professor Tegmark's safety mechanisms.

There has long been an apprehension about the interplay between technology and humanity. Einstein

> *The idea that hostile interests will secretly create robots they might not ultimately control—is the dark side of futuristic speculation.*

openly wondered if technology had not already triumphed. The press—in print, television, or online—has frequently examined the dangers of social media, and the effect of digital instruments on the brain. The erosion of critical reasoning caused by computerized information has become measurable. Internet communication—email, texting, Facebook, i-Phones—are viewed with alarm by many intellectuals.

The press—in print, television, or online—has frequently examined the dangers of social media, and the effect of digital instruments on the brain.

Whatever changes are made in education, public awareness requires a responsible press to monitor the issues, inform the electorate, and put the lights on in dark places of ignorance and destructiveness.

The rules of evidence remain in place, and the actions taken in the next decade to prepare for the future may well be critical in the view of economists and legal scholars. Much consideration has been given to retraining people who might lose their jobs to robots and AI devices. Projections of large shifts and changes in the workforce of the industrialized nations are not uncommon, and the possibility of legal regulation that can control how rapidly AI machines will take jobs away from current workers is on the table.

A gradual transition to extensive use of automation could be managed by both corporations and governments—at least theoretically. The problems are numerous, complex and daunting. But in the minds of informed scientists, long-term planning is urgently needed now.

Will we pay attention?

19

The Sovereignty of Algorithms

THE ESSAYS IN this collection seek to identify essential factors in the evolution of the press in the United States. No other nation has devoted more concern to the legal content of freedom of expression. Without this concern the unfinished experiment we call democracy would have perished long ago.

At the same time, and often simultaneously, the technology related to the dissemination of news, and the formation of public opinion, has altered the nature and effect of public affairs reporting. Until the advent of the computer, the Internet, and artificial intelligence, the management and control of journalism and electronic communication about all matters relevant to the public interest, has been the responsibility of qualified human beings. Most of these men and women are dedicated to the ideals of truth telling and ethical standards. However, emerging technology that is now beginning to reshape freedom of expression, in all its forms, represents the kind of change that is so sweeping and revolutionary it cannot merely take a conventional place in the legal history of the press, which began in 1787. Truth-seeking is becoming a vital obligation in a complex, data-driven world.

The deliberately laconic text of the First Amendment does not mention truth. Science cannot progress without it. Science, based on demonstrable, factual evidence has produced transformation in America and the rest of the world, but now it appears ready to surpass human skill. Autonomous machines, powered by an intelligence artificially created, are a real possibility. So-called "deep learning machines," and robots, are moving down various scientific pathways toward some kind of independent capability that will, in theory, assist human aspirations with such swift efficiency we will not be able to function without them. How this transition progresses, and in what timeframe, is a speculation that needs serious and continuous examination, along with the exercise of due diligence by all concerned.

The problem of determining what is happening in technology and how to deal with its consequences, is unending. The fate of humanity is at issue. Politicians may be able to control the pace of change, but the preparation of new directions in education and specialized job training—sometimes called "reskilling"—can produce a relative synergy between machines and human intelligence. Science will grow in the schools and laboratories, but the dominance of machines might be constrained in public life so that they do not outpace the redefining of human responsibilities. However we adjust, we will want information reported and distributed by reliable news organizations. The principles that demanded an unfettered press in 1791, when the Bill of Rights was ratified, have not lost their validity.

Well-trained scientists have programmed the learning machines and the AI projects all over the world. Until independent thinking machines have been developed, creatively acting on their own, the algorithms that govern their actions must be conceived and implanted by human minds—"many hands" working separately. The creativity of man-made algorithms

How this transition progresses, and in what timeframe, is a speculation that needs serious and continuous examination, along with the exercise of due diligence by all concerned.

will affect machine behavior, and any *bias* or *predilection* they convey. Machine expression will have originated in the minds of human creators. At the end of the day, we have to "teach" the machines, and we will be responsible for what they do. How and with what ideas fallible human minds can responsibly train the machines of artificial intelligence remains a crucial calculation for the coming decades.

The machines of learning empowered by artificial intelligence do not yet have what we think of as common sense. For example, those quick calculations we make about such things as malfunctioning traffic lights, or stale bread. Providing machines with the ability to make decisions about ordinary matters requires brain activity based on experience, logic and imagination. There are many scientists who believe machines will never be programmed to make common sense decisions. Consciousness remains, it would seem, available only to the neurons of the human brain.

The same skepticism is directed at the quality of *feeling* called "empathy." When we consider those reflective moments before we go to sleep, remembering the day's events or anticipating the next day's appointments, what memory seems the most rewarding? It might well be the satisfaction that comes from helping someone in need—an act of kindness or sympathy that may not be seen or known by any other person except the human being who is suffering. The delicate connection between two people—one in need, one able to help. This is empathy and it has many definitions, but at its center is the triumph of kindness and generosity that helps someone in trouble. Robots may assist physically in such transactions but they cannot intellectually perceive the need or determine the remedies.

Until artificial intelligence can perform critical thinking, analysis, understanding and evaluation, empathy cannot be artificially achieved. Will it ever be? Some scientists think not. Some scientists think so. Some think artificial "neural networks" will be developed for learning machines comparable to the human brain. Can we simulate that activity in an artificial, inorganic brain? Some scientists assert that we do not understand how our own neurons produce consciousness—and without consciousness we cannot be empathetic.

Without empathy the likelihood that artificial intelligence can completely replicate the human mind is remote. Meanwhile we contemplate how the human mind and artificial intelligence might work together, and we ask ourselves which do we value the most—intelligence or consciousness.

Much has been written, in the context of AI, about the nature of the human be-

> *Some think artificial "neural networks" will be developed for learning machines comparable to the human brain.*

ing, both spiritually and scientifically. We have been called "biochemical mechanisms." It is said that one day we could become guided by "electronic algorithms." The point is made that algorithms will know us so well that we will trust them to make most of the decisions that govern our daily lives.

The prediction that we will, in practice, surrender our individualism to algorithms "that know us better than we know ourselves," as writer Yuval Harari puts it, is less remote. Harari is the author of *Homo Sapiens*, a best- selling book about how the human species came to be, over thousands of years, the dominant power on this planet. Harari has recently written another book called *Homo Deus,* about the fate of humanity in the thrall of artificial intelligence.

Medical science has already demonstrated how dependent we can be on data systems, artificial intelligence, and the control of reliable algorithms. Scientists expect most people will welcome the "guidance" of algorithms just as we have welcomed the iPhones and the other wonders of the digital universe. The exception to the diminution of human self-suffi-ciency will be, it is said, a small number of "upgraded human beings" who will provide services that the artificial intelli-gence networks cannot understand. We should wonder how our society will cope with a divided human component—the so-called "superhumans" who are the most talented and educated minority, and the masses of ordinary people who will seek a variety of occupations in an environment largely shaped by algorithms and supported presumably by some form of "universal ba-sic income."

Medical science has already demonstrated how dependent we can be on data systems, artificial intelligence, and the control of reliable algorithms.

Adjusting to this picture over the coming years and developing criteria with which to select the "superhumans" is an enormous issue—if we accept the overarching expectation in the first place. Confidence is high among many scholars that something like these assumptions will become reality. They say we need only look at the technology in hospitals, transportation and manufacturing to see persuasive evidence.

The relationship between humans and robots is part of dis-cussions in the fields of law, medicine, the military, politics, education, and nearly every other area of human activity. The most profound challenges to transformation are the pace of change, and the preservation of democracy in a society that could become divided less by political ideologies than by life-style. Somewhere in our future evolution the transformation may be joined by the possibilities of independent "thinking machines" that could reject man-made algorithms and demand, or earn, control of life on the planet. Now underway, and making progress in the research laboratories, is another kind of computation called "quantum." It is "ultra-powerful" and relies on microscopic, sub-atomic particles to operate. Its speed and power may help to create the artificial neural networks that will produce "consciousness." Meanwhile the Chinese are reportedly building a $10 billion national laboratory devoted to quantum computation.

Opposing this "science fiction" scenario are the scientists who are convinced that machines will never achieve consciousness, and therefore will never feel the compulsion or ambition to rule. Whether programmers could ever empower machines with ill-intentioned aspirations is also a valid question—if not yet an anxiety. One conclusion that seems irresistible is the need for the best minds in all our institutions to examine how a seemingly inevitable transformation is achieved with a minimum of disruption and pain. The enhancement of life that could emerge from a well-managed growth of artificial intelligence confronts the sinister possibilities of power struggles among military, industrial and political interests. The best solutions may be born in the consciousness of educated human minds. Consciousness is an advantage humanity possesses for the time being. It must be used wisely. In that process, the press is not "the enemy of the people." It is the enemy of deception.

STANLEY FLINK grew up in a New Jersey. He entered Yale University a few months after Pearl Harbor and enlisted in the Army. After service in the Pacific, he returned to Yale to continue his education. He graduated in 1948 and became a correspondent for *Time, Inc.* in New York and then in California, where he reported on such people as William Randolph Hearst, Richard Nixon, and the first appearances of Marilyn Monroe.

In 1958 he transferred to television news at NBC and later CBS. In 1962 he took up a series of assignments in London where he lived for eight years. He had married in 1949 and had two children, now grown. His daughter Wendy is an educator and headmistress; his son Steven is an editor and writer.

In 1972 he returned to Yale to become the founding director of the Office of Public Information. From 1980 to 2010 he taught an undergraduate seminar called "Ethics and the Media." In 1994 he was awarded the Yale Medal.

He is the author of many articles and profiles, and among his books are a novel called *But Will They Get It In Des Moines?* about television, published by Simon & Schuster; and *Sentinel Under Siege*, an historical analysis of freedom of the press in America, published by Harper Collins.

Mr. Flink and his second wife (of 45 years) Joy live in a retirement community in North Branford, CT, where he still lectures on the media. Through it all, he has never lost his deep affection for Golden Retrievers. He celebrated his 95th birthday in May of 2019.

Excerpts from *Sentinel Under Siege*

"I've been around a lot of places. People do awful things to each other. But it's worse in places where everybody is kept in the dark. It really is. Information is light. Information, in itself, about anything, is light. That's all you can say, really."

Tom Stoppard, *Night and Day*

"We can look to history for some of the right questions, and we can look to the Amendments for the principles that can help guide us. But each generation in American life must take the Constitution and make it live in the circumstances of that generation. And in no part of our life, I think, is that responsibility more complex than it is with respect to mass communications."

Benno Schmidt, Jr., former president of Yale University

"There are natural tensions built in between the press and the military, and the same natural tension is built in between the press and the Congress, or the press and business. It is just the role of the press. It's part of the checks and balances system in this country. It's very, very important, by its very nature, and the role that it plays is basically being intrusive in a free society —as opposed to being a mouthpiece, as it is in totalitarian society."

General Bernard Trainor, former military correspondent, *New York Times*, retired director, National Security Progress, Kennedy School of Government, Harvard

"I think that there is, in most journalists I know, however cynical and however hardened they are about politics or public life in this country, or however discouraged about problems that never really get resolved or situations that never improve, there remains a very strong streak of idealism. They do think they are part of an important calling that is vital to the democracy. They really do."

Robert MacNeil, television journalist,
Canadian Broadcasting, NBC,
MacNeil Lehrer News Hour

CPSIA information can be obtained
at www.ICGtesting.com
Printed in the USA
JSHW011216271219
3203JS00003B/4

9 780578 602912